AF765230

WORDPERFECT® PRESENTATIONS™

SOUTH-WESTERN

WORDPERFECT® PRESENTATIONS™ 3.0 FOR WINDOWS®

QUICK COURSE

Teri Goldfarb
UNIVERSITY OF CINCINNATI
RAYMOND WALTERS COLLEGE

Donna Jagodzinski

Catherine Skintik

SOUTH-WESTERN EDUCATIONAL PUBLISHING

I(T)P™

International Thomson Publishing

South-Western Educational Publishing is a division of International Thomson Publishing, Inc. The ITP trademark is used under license.

ISBN: 0-538-64909-7
1 2 3 4 5 6 H 00 99 98 97 96 95
Printed in the United States of America

Editor-in-Chief:	Bob First
Managing Editor:	Janie F. Schwark
Developmental Editor:	Dave Lafferty
Production:	Custom Editorial Productions, Inc.
Art Director:	John Robb
Consulting Editor:	Custom Editorial Productions, Inc.

Preface

TO THE STUDENT

Presentation graphics is a relatively new field in computer software applications. Though you may know several software programs such as word processing programs or spreadsheet programs, you may have little familiarity with presentation graphics. *WordPerfect Presentations 3.0 for Windows: Quick Course* is designed to introduce you not only to the Presentations software but to the concepts involved with planning and organizing a presentation.

WordPerfect Presentations is a software program designed to help you create effective visual presentations. Using Presentations, you can create slide presentations, overhead transparencies, printed handouts, and screen shows on the computer screen. Presentation graphics can help you perform almost any task that involves communicating your ideas to a group.

Even if you have little experience using computers, you will find *WordPerfect Presentations 3.0 for Windows: Quick Course* easy to use. You will receive a solid grounding in Windows basics, you will learn how to plan a presentation before creating it in Presentations, and you will learn how to create sophisticated and exciting slide shows.

ABOUT THIS BOOK

WordPerfect Presentations 3.0 for Windows: Quick Course provides you with a complete learning package that will make your mastery of the Presentations software both easy and fun. Objectives listed at the beginning of each lesson indicate the subjects you will be covering. Each concept is introduced by discussions that explain the concept and outline the steps you will be practicing. Exercises follow to allow you to practice the new concept in a real-world application. Illustrations point out important parts of the Presentations screens and allow you to evaluate your work as you go along. End-of-lesson activities and review exercises give you the opportunity to review material you have learned in each lesson. Each lesson includes a suggested completion time, but actual completion time depends on ability and computer experience. Most students should be able to complete the course in 12 hours.

A template disk is available for use with this book. Template files give you a head start in preparing some presentations so that you can master concepts rapidly.

SYSTEM REQUIREMENTS

WordPerfect Presentations has the following system requirements:

- Microsoft Windows version 3.1 or later, and Microsoft MS-DOS version 3.1 or later
- 80386 or higher microprocessor
- 4 megabytes (MB) of memory
- 3.5-inch high-density disk drive
- Approximately 10.5 MB of space free on hard disk for minimum installation; 24 MB for complete installation
- A Video Graphics Array (VGA) display or better
- Mouse
- To print, any Windows-supported printer

ACKNOWLEDGMENTS

I would like to acknowledge the following for their invaluable help in completing this project: My husband Ed, whose steadfast support (and willingness to let me spend our vacation working on this project) kept me going; my friend Stan Thompson, whose faith in my ability gave me the confidence I needed to take on this project; my editor Cat Skintik, whose guidance and expert suggestions produced a book that far surpasses its original form; and always, the constant help from the One Who Makes All Things Possible.

Donna Jagodzinski

Table of Contents

GETTING STARTED

Getting Started with WordPerfect Presentations

OBJECTIVES

After completing this lesson, you will be able to:

1. Discuss presentation graphics.
2. Start WordPerfect Presentations.
3. Communicate with Presentations.
4. Use the menu bar and the Toolbar.
5. Open and close files.
6. Play a slide show.
7. Exit Presentations.

Estimated Time: 3/4 hour

INTRODUCTION

Presentation graphics, software programs designed to help you create effective visual presentations, allow you to create slide presentations, overhead transparencies, printed handouts, and screen shows on the computer screen. Presentation graphics can help you explain, persuade, teach, sell, and inform. In fact, presentation graphics can help you perform almost any task that involves communicating your ideas to a group. The Presentations graphics program provides text and graphics tools, as well as preformatted tables, charts, and graphs, to help you create winning presentations.

STARTING PRESENTATIONS

You start Presentations from the Program Manager in Windows. To start Presentations, you must first locate the Presentations *icon.*

NOTE

An icon is a small picture that represents a command or activity.

By default, the Presentations icon is located in a program group called *Presentations* or *Novell PerfectOffice*. However, because Windows lets you customize your program groups, the icon could be located elsewhere on your PC. If you have trouble locating the Presentations icon, ask your instructor for assistance.

Presentations

EXERCISE GS-1

This exercise assumes you have started Windows and located the Presentations icon.

1. Open Presentations by *double-clicking* on its icon. The Document Selection dialog box appears, as shown in Figure GS–1.

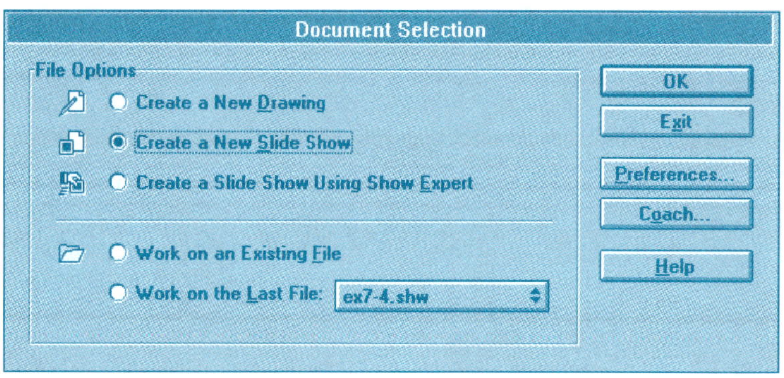

Figure GS–1
The Document Selection dialog box

The Document Selection dialog box is your doorway into Presentations. You use this box to tell Presentations what you want to do: create a new drawing, create a new slide show, create a slide show using Show Expert, or work on an existing file.

2. For now, *click* on the **OK** button. The New Slide Show dialog box appears, as shown in Figure GS–2.
3. Leave this dialog box on the screen for the next exercise.

NOTE

Clicking means pressing and quickly releasing the left mouse button. Double-clicking means clicking twice rapidly.

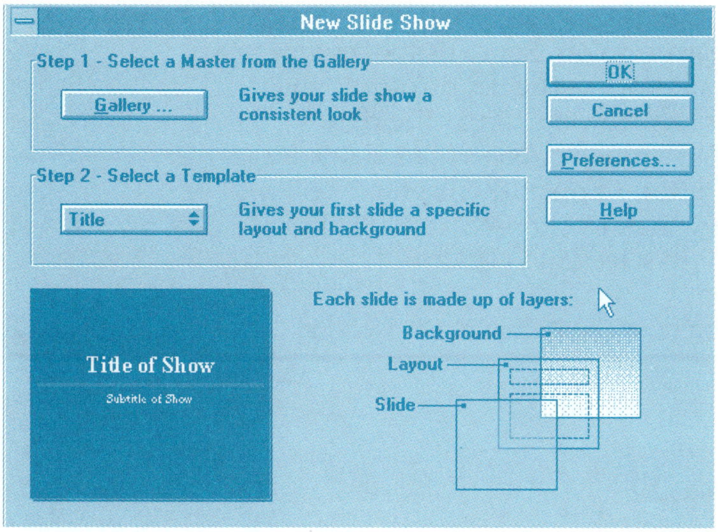

Figure GS–2
The New Slide Show dialog box

COMMUNICATING WITH PRESENTATIONS

As you work with a slide show, you need to choose among the options Presentations offers. For example, the New Slide Show dialog box now on your screen gives you several choices about how to set up your new slide show.

Dialog boxes appear when Presentations needs more information from you before completing an action. Dialog boxes can contain command buttons, option buttons, check boxes, text boxes, and list boxes. These items let you give Presentations specific instructions about how to operate.

Command buttons are rectangular buttons with labels such as OK, Cancel, Help, and so on. To choose a command button:

- Move the mouse pointer to the button you want to choose.
- Click the left mouse button.

Mouse Pointer

N O T E

The mouse pointer looks like an arrowhead.

You can select only one command button at a time.

Option buttons are small round buttons, sometimes called "radio buttons." You can select only one option button at a time.

Check boxes are small square boxes that appear next to certain menu options. Select as many check boxes as you need. If an item is dimmed, it is not available.

To choose option buttons or check boxes:

- Click on the button or box you want to choose.
- Click on the option or box again to *deselect* it.

Text boxes require you to key information. This is often the only way to enter some kinds of information. A blinking vertical line, called the *cursor*, indicates the insertion point where you can add or delete text.

A *list box* contains a list of text items that refer to files, devices (for example, disk drives), formats, and so on. Some list boxes are always displayed; sometimes you cannot see the list box until you open it. When a text box includes an arrow button at the right side, it means a list box with predetermined choices is available for the text box. Click on the arrow button to open the list box. Because there are several items from which to choose in any list box, simply point to the item you want to select and click.

EXERCISE GS-2

Click **OK** in the New Slide Show dialog box. The Presentations working screen appears.

WORKING WITH THE PRESENTATIONS SCREEN

Look carefully at the Presentations screen. Some features of this screen are common to many Windows applications, while others are found only in Presentations. The most important features are labeled in Figure GS–3.

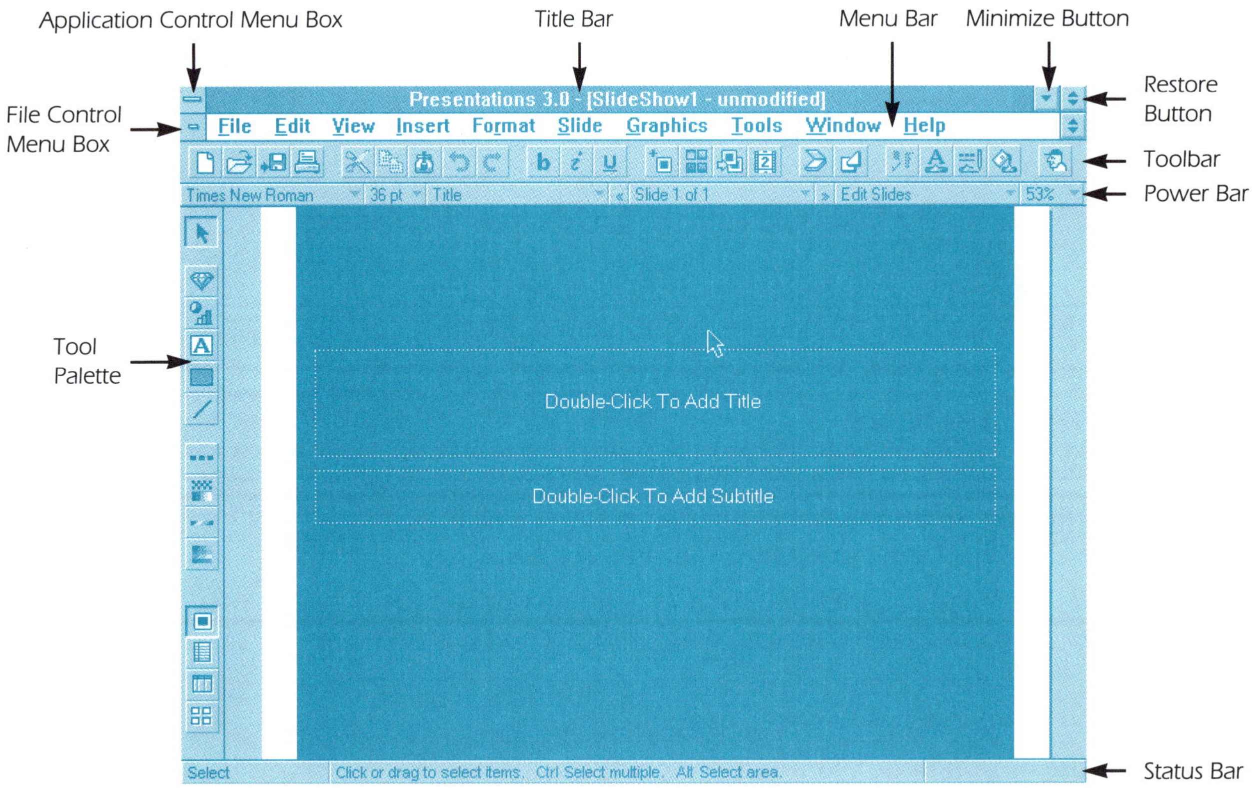

Figure GS–3
Features of the Presentations screen

The Menu Bar and the Toolbar

The *menu bar* lists currently available *menus*. Menus are lists of commands that Presentations can carry out.

To select items from the menu bar:

- Move the mouse pointer to the name of the menu you want to use, then click. A list of menu items drops down, showing the commands currently available.
- Click on the command you want to select.
- To remove a menu without making a choice, click elsewhere on the screen.

The *Toolbar* is a collection of small pictures, or icons, that represent some of the most frequently used menu commands. These Toolbar icons provide shortcuts that can speed up your work. If you leave your mouse pointer on a Toolbar icon, a label will appear to tell you what the icon does.

To choose a command from the Toolbar, point to the command icon and click.

The Power Bar and the Tool Palette

The *Power Bar* appears directly below the Toolbar. It contains a series of buttons you use to control current settings and screen views (see Figure GS–4). To choose an option from the Power Bar, click on the desired button. A list drops down, offering you further choices.

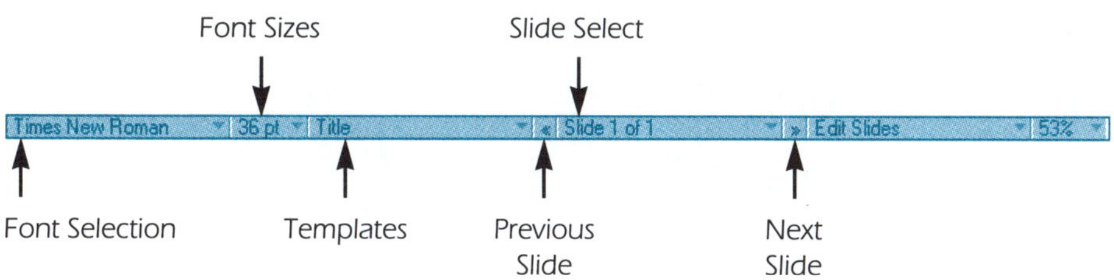

Figure GS–4
The Power Bar

The *tool palette*, located at the left side of the screen, provides you with icons representing tools and other options that also appear on menus. As you become more familiar with Presentations, you will find using the tool palette easier and faster than using menus.

The Working Screen

Figure GS–5 (on p. 6) shows a close-up of the Presentations working screen. As a general rule, the working screen consists of a *background* and various kinds of boxes where you can add text, tables, drawings, or charts. You can change the background to any one of 66 choices, or you can choose to have no background. The boxes supplied vary according to the type of slide you are working on.

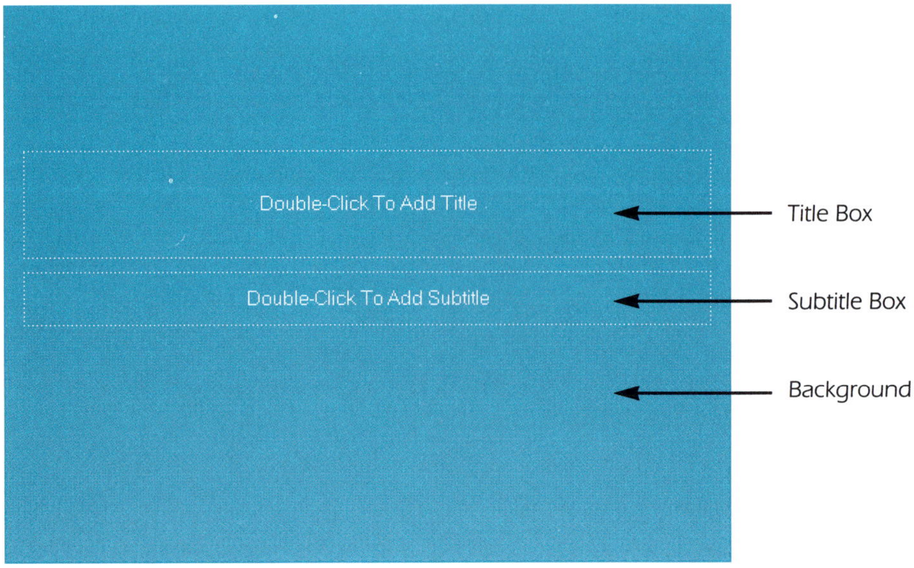

Figure GS–5
The Presentations working screen, showing background, title box, and subtitle box

▶ EXERCISE GS–3

Practice using the menu bar and the Toolbar.

1. Choose **File** and examine the commands available on this menu.
2. Click elsewhere on the screen to remove the menu.
3. Select the **Open** icon from the Toolbar. The Open File dialog box shown in Figure GS–6 appears.

Open

4. Leave the Open File dialog box on the screen for the next exercise.

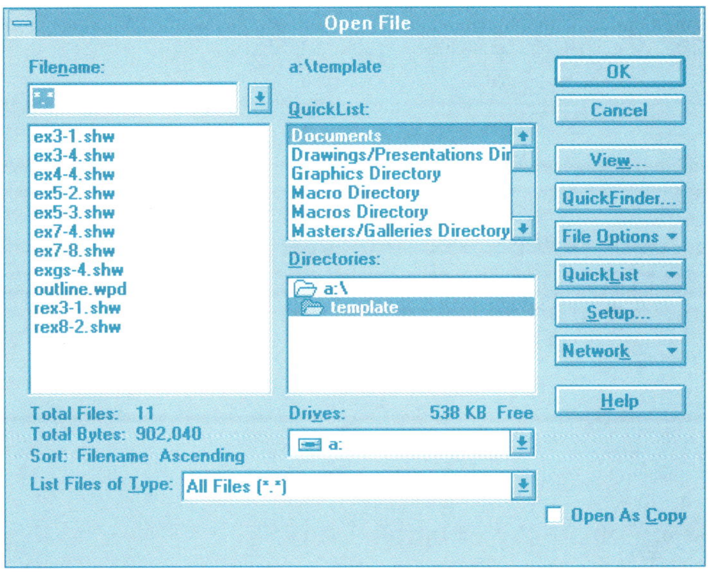

Figure GS–6
The Open File dialog box

OPENING A FILE

As you work with Presentations, you will need to know how to open slide shows or other files. *Opening* a file means retrieving the file from the location where it is stored.

The Open File dialog box, currently on your screen, lets you find the file you need and open it for use. The Drives box, located at the bottom right of the dialog box, lets you choose the drive that contains the file. The Directories box shows you what directories are located on the current drive. Files that are available in the selected directory appear in the Filename list box.

To open a document:

- Choose **Open** from the **File** menu.
  or
- Select the **Open** icon from the Toolbar.

To open a file from a floppy disk:

- First insert the disk.
- In the Drives box, click on the drive letter of the drive where you inserted the disk.

To find a file in a directory:

- Double-click on the directory's folder in the Directories box.
- Click on the name of the file in the Filename box.
- Click **OK.**

EXERCISE GS-4

Open a file from the template disk.

1. Insert your template disk in drive A or B as required.
2. Choose **a:** or **b:** as required in the Drives box.
3. Click on **EXGS-4.SHW** in the Filename list.
4. Click **OK.**
5. Leave the slide show on the screen for the next exercise.

PLAYING A SLIDE SHOW

The *slide show* currently on your screen is made up of five slides used to illustrate a presentation. After you create your slide show, you can play it directly on your computer screen. To play a slide show:

- Choose **Play Slide Show** from the **Slide** menu.
  This displays the Play Slide Show dialog box (see Figure GS–7, on p. 8).
- Choose the **Play Show** icon from the Toolbar.
  or
- To begin playing the show, choose the **Play** command button.

Play Show

You use the Play Slide Show dialog box to control the slide show. In this dialog box, you can specify which slide you want to start with and you can set the slide show to automatically repeat.

Figure GS–7
The Play Slide Show dialog box

When the slide show starts, click the left mouse button to move forward through the slides, or the right mouse button to back up to a previous slide.

EXERCISE GS–5

Play the slide show on your screen.

1. Choose **Play Slide Show** from the **Slide** menu.
2. Choose **Play** in the **Play Slide Show** dialog box.
3. Click the left mouse button to advance through the slides. When you have reached the end of the slide show, Presentations redisplays the working screen.
4. Leave the slide show on the screen for the next exercise.

CLOSING A FILE

Closing a file removes the document from the screen.

To close a file:

- Choose **Close** from the **File** menu.

  or
- Double-click on the document's Control menu box. (Refer back to Figure GS–3 for the location of the Control menu box.)

After you close the last open file for your current session, the Document Selection dialog box appears. You can then choose to work further in Presentations or exit the program.

EXERCISE GS–6

Close the file on your screen.

1. Choose **Close** from the **File** menu.
2. Leave the Document Selection dialog box on the screen for the next exercise.

EXITING PRESENTATIONS

To stop working with Presentations:

- Choose **Exit** from the **File** menu.

  or

- Click on the **Exit** command button in the Document Selection dialog box.

EXERCISE GS-7

Click on the **Exit** button in the Document Selection dialog box to exit Presentations.

ACTIVITIES

TRUE/FALSE

In the blank space before each sentence, place a **T** if the statement is true and an **F** if it is false.

______ 1. The first thing you see when you start Presentations is the working screen.

______ 2. You can select only one command button at a time.

______ 3. Once you open a menu, you must make a selection from it.

______ 4. To retrieve a file you want to work with, use the Open File dialog box.

______ 5. The Toolbar is located at the left side of the working screen.

COMPLETION

Fill in the blank.

1. ________________ help you create effective visual presentations.
2. A small picture that represents a command or activity is a/an

   ________________.
3. You use the ________________ dialog box to tell Presentations what you want to do when you start the program.
4. ________________ are also called radio buttons.
5. The ________________ is a series of buttons you can use to control current settings and screen views.

LESSON 1

Planning and Creating Your First Presentation

OBJECTIVES

After completing this lesson, you will be able to:

1. Understand the purpose and goals of presentations.
2. Create a presentation in the Outliner.
3. Save a slide show.
4. Import or export an outline.

Estimated Time: 1 hour

INTRODUCTION

To create a successful presentation, you must carefully plan what you want to accomplish with this presentation and how you will go about accomplishing it. Use the following steps to do this:

- Set your objectives—Determine what you are trying to accomplish with this presentation.
- Gather your information—Research your topic thoroughly.
- Organize your information—Examine carefully the information you have gathered and determine how to present it.
- Create an outline—Use the outline to create the visuals (slides) you will present to your audience.
- Prepare your text—Create the slides you will be presenting and determine what you will say during your presentation.

PLANNING YOUR PRESENTATION

Every presentation has a purpose. It might be selling a product, explaining a concept, or distributing information. If you want your presentation to be successful, the first step in your planning process should be clearly defining that purpose. The time you spend planning your layout and supporting materials can guarantee the success of your work.

Setting Objectives

You start planning a presentation by defining your objectives. Following are some objectives or combinations of objectives you might be trying to accomplish in your presentation:

- Inform and/or answer questions.
- Change an opinion or gain acceptance.
- Persuade others to take some sort of action.
- Arouse interest.
- Evaluate or clarify.
- Make recommendations.

Once you have finished writing your objectives, read and reread them to make sure they express exactly what you want to include in your presentation.

Gathering and Organizing Information

Next, gather and organize the information you want to convey. To obtain information that will assist in your preparation, use all of the sources available to you. The library is a good place to start collecting relevant data.

How you organize your material depends on its content. The most frequently used format is sequential or chronological—that is, discuss items in the order in which they occur. Another way to organize the information is in order of importance of the data. No matter how you decide to organize your material, the "secrets" to a successful presentation are:

- When you introduce your subject, tell your audience what you're going to talk about so they will be focused on what follows.
- When you talk about your subject, make sure your presentation contains sufficient information to "sell" the audience.
- When you summarize what you have told the audience, briefly touch on your main points so the memory of the presentation will remain with them.

Creating the Outline

Now you can begin to design your presentation to meet the specific objectives you have listed. To help with this part of your task, you can write an outline to help create the skeleton of your presentation.

As you work on your outline, sort the information you want to include into three categories:

1. Information essential to your presentation (usually the main headings of your outline).
2. Supporting information that makes your presentation more believable (usually the subheadings of your outline). Supporting information can include data and visuals that relate to your topic.
3. Information that enhances your presentation but is not essential (usually the sub-subheadings of your outline).

You should have at least two headings in a presentation and at least two subheadings under a main heading. Sub-subheadings are not required.

You can use the traditional outline format shown in Figure 1–1 (on p. 16) as a guide for an informative presentation. You can adapt this outline for your own presentations, whatever your goals might be.

Preparing the Text

To create an effective slide show, you should master two skills for preparing text. First, condense your ideas into manageable phrases on a slide by *eliminating unnecessary words*. Second, don't try to convey more than one idea in a phrase.

When you create slides, keep the wording concise. Eliminate unnecessary words, phrases, and punctuation. The object of your presentation is to get your message across. Unnecessary words can

I.	Title of presentation	
	A.	Attention-getting material
		Captures audience interest
	B.	Orienting material
		Provides information necessary for the rest of the presentation
II.	Problem or proposal	
	A.	First main point
		Examples, illustrations, statistics, or explanations
	B.	Second main point
		Examples, illustrations, statistics, or explanations
III.	Conclusion	
	A.	Summary
	B.	Restatement of original goal

Figure 1–1
A sample outline

make slides difficult to read and understand. However, you can occasionally repeat words to show emphasis.

The structure of your headings should be grammatically parallel. This means that they use the same grammatical structure. For example, if you use a sentence fragment for the first heading, all headings should be sentence fragments. Subheadings can use a different structure, but all subheadings should be parallel with each other. The following examples show correct and incorrect parallel structure:

Parallel Headings	**Nonparallel Headings**
Look Smart	Try to Look Smart
Act Smart	You Can Act Smart
Be Smart	Being Smart Is Important

Visual elements allow the audience to scan information and recognize the information you have selected as important. Some of the most common visual elements are indentations, font (typeface) selection, and font style. Indenting visually organizes the material for your audience. Font choice affects how your audience perceives your message, because some fonts are more formal than others. Bold or italic font style helps you add emphasis.

You want your audience to grasp your ideas, but you do not want to overwhelm them with what they see. Use concise, effective visuals to express your message.

CREATING OUTLINES WITH THE PRESENTATIONS OUTLINER

Presentations offers a screen view called the *Outliner* that can help you create your outline. The outline you create in the Outliner then automatically becomes a slide show.

To enter Outliner:

- Select **Outliner** from the **View** menu.

  or

- Click on the **Outliner View** icon in the tool palette.

The screen changes to resemble a piece of lined notebook paper (Figure 1–2).

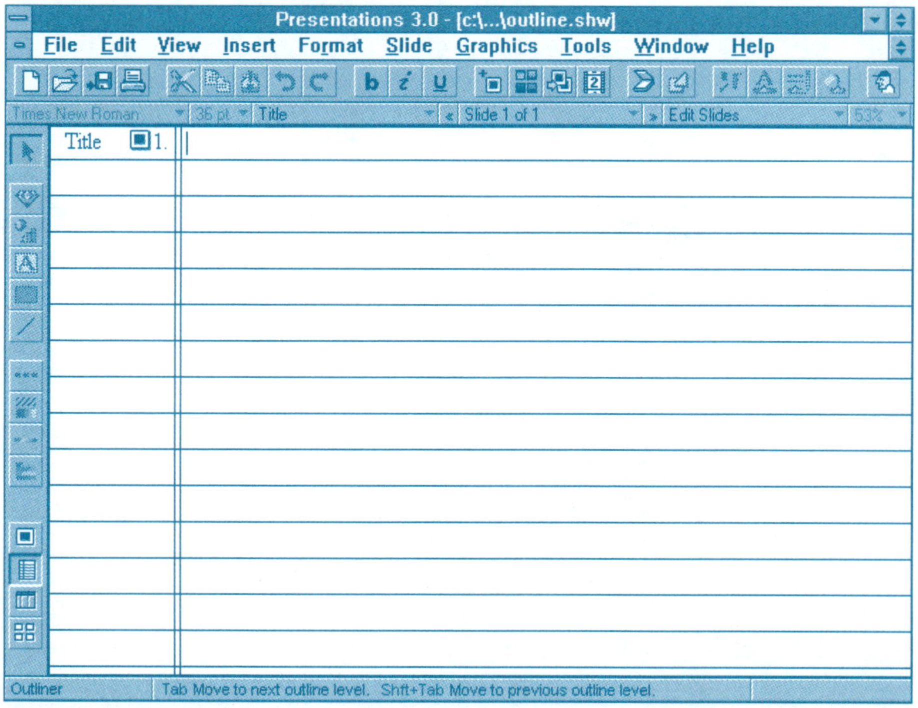

Figure 1–2
The Outliner window

The Outliner indicates levels of text to the left of the double vertical rule. You key entries to the right of the rules. The slide icon next to the number *1* tells you Presentations is ready for you to enter the information for your first slide. When you enter Outliner, Presentations assumes you will begin the new slide with a title, so the first line is designated *Title*.

To create your outline, key your first title on the first line. Press Enter to move to the next line. The Outliner assumes that your next line will be a subtitle. The word *Subtitle* appears in the left margin and the cursor automatically moves to the right to show an indent under the title. After you have entered a subtitle, pressing Enter again will take you to a line designated as *Text*. Use this line for supporting material, examples, illustrations, and so on. The Outliner will assume that every time you press Enter at this level, you are inserting additional text. The indent stays constant under the *Subtitle* line. To begin creating a new slide and enter a new title, press Shift+Tab.

You use the Tab key to indent further to the right. If, for example, your outline has no subtitle following a title, but does have text, press Tab once to change the Subtitle line to a Text line. You can indent Text lines further by pressing Tab additional times. Press Shift+Tab to move back to the left one level at a time, until you reach the Title level once more.

As you create the outline, remember that you are preparing a series of slides. Each slide can have only one title and one subtitle, but it can have several lines of text. Each heading level appears in a specific location on the slide, as shown in Figure 1–3.

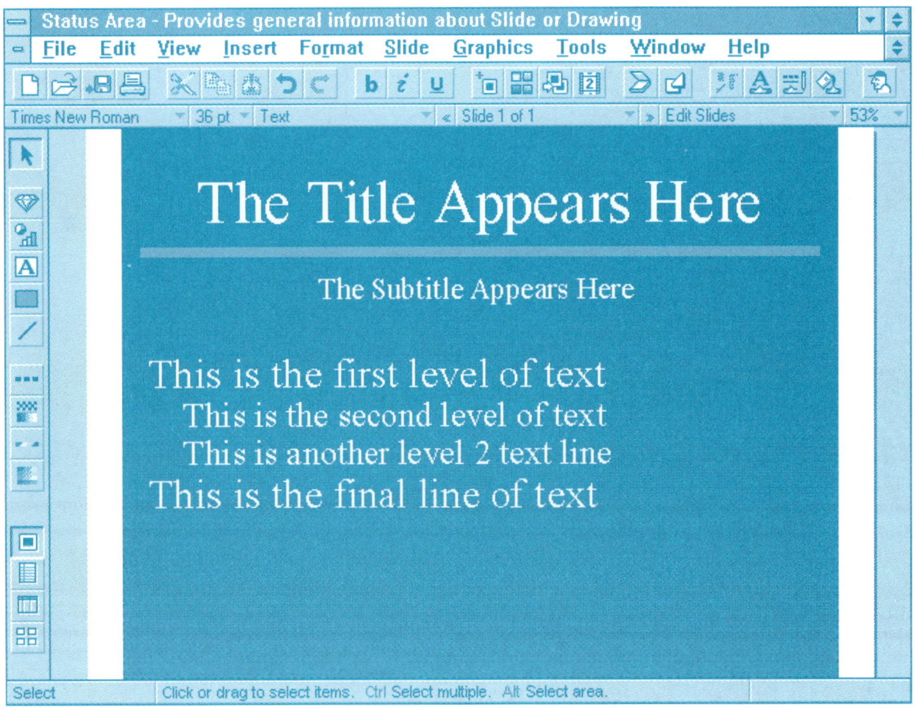

Figure 1–3
A sample slide showing how Title, Subtitle, and Text entries appear

To correct errors in the outline, click the mouse pointer to locate the cursor where you want to make a correction. Use Backspace or Delete to remove text, then key the correct text.

EXERCISE 1-1

In this exercise, you create an outline describing the features of an ice cream company's products.

1. Start Presentations. Click on **OK** in the Document Selection and New Slide Show dialog boxes.
2. In the Presentations working screen, select **Outliner** from the **View** menu to start the Outliner.

3. On the first line (*Title*), key **The ShurSweet Ice Cream Company** and press **Enter.**
4. The cursor appears on the next line (*Subtitle*). Key **Wholesale Premium Ice Cream** and press **Enter.**
5. You have now completed the first slide. Press **Shift+Tab** to create a second Title line. The left margin area will show that you are ready to create Slide 2.
6. Enter the title of Slide 2. Key **It's Affordable** and press **Enter.**
7. Enter the subtitle for Slide 2. Key **Bulk Prices for Large Orders** and press **Enter.**
8. Press **Shift+Tab** to create a third Title line.
9. Using the instructions above, create three more slides using the following information:

Slide 3	Title:	**It's Convenient**
	Subtitle:	**Wide Variety of Flavors**
Slide 4	Title:	**It's Delicious**
	Subtitle:	**#1 Rating in Taste Surveys**
Slide 5	Title:	**ShurSweet Ice Cream**
	Subtitle:	**The Right Choice!**

10. Your screen should resemble Figure 1–4. Check your entries and fix any errors you find.
11. Leave the outline on the screen for the next exercise.

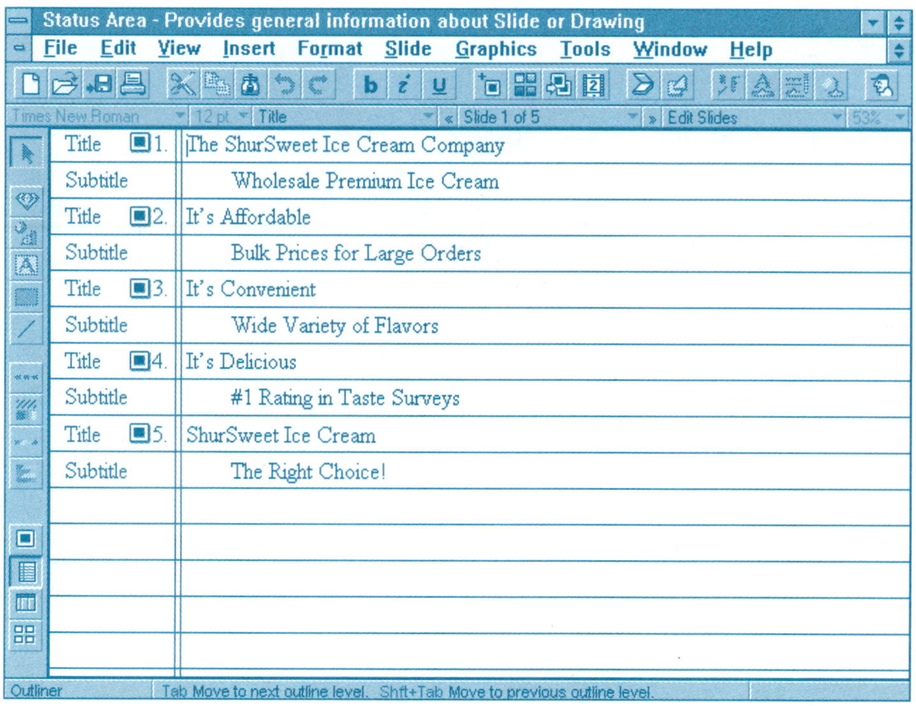

Figure 1–4
The completed outline

SAVING THE PRESENTATION

When you save your work for the first time, Presentations displays the Save dialog box, where you can name your presentation and select the drive and directory where you want to store the presentation.

When Presentations saves the file, it adds a three-letter extension (for a slide show, **.SHW**) to the name you specified. After that, when you use the Save command to save your work, Presentations saves your presentation on top of your original document. If you want to retain the original document, use the Save As command. In the Save As dialog box, you can give the document a new name or save it to a different directory or drive.

Presentations by default saves documents to the Presentations **FILES** subdirectory. To save a file in a different location, choose the desired drive from the Drives list box and choose the appropriate directory from the Directories list box.

NOTE

For this course, you will save all files on your data disk.

To save a document:

- Choose **Save** from the **File** menu.
  or
- Click the **Save** icon on the Toolbar.

Save

- In the Filename text box, key a name for the file (from one to eight characters long).
- If necessary, choose a different drive or directory to store the file.
- Click **OK.**

EXERCISE 1-2

Save and then play the slide show you created in Exercise 1–1.

1. Insert your data disk into drive A or B as required.
2. Choose **Save** from the **File** menu.
3. In the Filename text box, key **SHUROUTL.**
4. In the Drives list box, select the drive into which you inserted the data disk.
5. Click on the **OK** button to save the file.
6. Place the cursor on the first line of the outline. Choose **Play Slide Show** from the **Slide** menu, then click on the **Play** button and view each slide created in the Outliner.
7. When you have finished playing the slide show, close it.
8. Leave the Document Selection dialog box on the screen for the next exercise.

IMPORTING AND EXPORTING OUTLINES

Occasionally, you might want to use an outline you created in another application as the basis for a Presentations slide show. For example, you might want to use an outline you created in WordPerfect or another word processor.

Importing an Outline

You can import into Presentations an outline created in WordPerfect. The outline must be created with WordPerfect's Outline feature.

To import an outline:

- Choose **File** from the **Insert** menu. The Insert Outline dialog box appears.
- Select the name of the file you want to import and click **Insert.**

EXERCISE 1-3

Import a WordPerfect outline.

1. Click on **OK** in the Document Selection dialog box and in the New Slide Show dialog box to open a new slide show.
2. Choose **Outliner** from the **View** menu. A blank outline window appears.
3. To import an outline created in WordPerfect:
   a. Insert your template disk into drive A or B, as required.
   b. Choose **File** from the **Insert** menu. The Insert Outline dialog box appears.
   c. Change to drive A or B, as required.
   d. Click on **OUTLINE.WPD,** then click on the **Insert** button.
4. The outline appears in the Outliner.
5. Leave the document on the screen for the next exercise.

NOTE

You might need to select All Files from the List Files of Type list box at the bottom of the Insert Outline dialog box to display the name of the WordPerfect file in the Filename list.

Exporting an Outline with the Clipboard

You can use the clipboard to export an outline to a word processing program. The *clipboard* is a storage area in memory common to all Windows applications. You use the clipboard to move or copy data from one place or document to another. *Moving* means removing data from one location and placing it in another location. *Copying* means placing a duplicate of the selected data in another location, while leaving the original data intact.

To move data from one location to another:

- Click and drag to select the data you want to move.
- Choose **Cut** from the **Edit** menu.
- Click on the location where you want to insert the data.
- Select **Paste** from the **Edit** menu.

To place a *copy* of data in another location, and leave the original data intact:

- Click and drag to select the data you want to copy.
- Choose **Copy** from the **Edit** menu.
- Click on the location where you want to insert the copy.
- Choose **Paste** from the **Edit** menu.

NOTE

You can also use the Cut, Copy, and Paste commands to move and copy text in any Presentations screen.

The information you cut or copy is stored in the clipboard until you store something else on top of it or until you turn the computer off. You can insert multiple copies of data by selecting Paste repeatedly.

EXERCISE 1-4

Export the outline on your screen.

1. Highlight the entire outline by dragging from the left side of the first line to the last line of the outline.
2. Choose **Cut** from the **Edit** menu. The entire document is deleted from the screen and copied into the clipboard.
3. Minimize Presentations by clicking on the upside-down triangle in the upper right corner of the window.

Minimize

4. Open the **WordPerfect** program group in the Program Manager.
5. Double-click on the **WordPerfect** icon to open WordPerfect.
6. Choose **Paste** from the **Edit** menu. The outline appears in the WordPerfect window.
7. Choose **Exit** from the **File** menu to exit WordPerfect. When WordPerfect asks if you want to save changes, click on **No**.
8. Restore Presentations (double-click on the **Presentations** icon at the bottom of your screen).
9. Close the file without saving and exit Presentations.

ACTIVITIES

TRUE/FALSE

In the blank space before each sentence, place a **T** if the statement is true and an **F** if it is false.

______ 1. The first step in planning your presentation is gathering information.

______ 2. You should organize your material based on its content.

______ 3. Parallel headings use the same grammatical structure.

______ 4. You use the Cut and Paste commands to copy data to a new location.

______ 5. After you create an outline in the Outliner, you must then create slides for the presentation.

COMPLETION

Fill in the blank.

1. You start planning a presentation by defining your ________________.
2. You can use the ________________ to export an outline.
3. You should have at least ________________ headings in a presentation.
4. The ________________ view resembles a piece of lined notebook paper.
5. You use the ________________ option to store a revised file in a location different from the original.

REVIEW

REVIEW EXERCISE 1-1

In this exercise, you will create an outline for a presentation.

1. Choose a topic from the list below, or use a topic of your own.
    - Skiing advice for novices.
    - Housetraining a new puppy.
    - Using a word processor for homework assignments.
    - Making chocolate chip cookies.
    - Working out.
2. Following the guidelines in this lesson, decide how you would make a presentation on your topic. Write a title (and a subtitle, if desired) for your presentation.
3. Write an outline on paper of your presentation. Set up your outline as it would appear in the Presentations Outliner, using titles, subtitles, and text entries.
4. Check your outline to make sure you have suitable headings, subheadings, and supporting information. Make sure your entries follow the guidelines for preparing text and using parallel grammar presented in this lesson.
5. If desired, go on to the next exercise.

REVIEW EXERCISE 1-2

Enter your outline from Review Exercise 1–1 into the Outliner.

1. Start Presentations. In the Document Selection and New Slide Show dialog boxes, click **OK.**
2. In the Presentations working screen, choose **Outliner** from the **View** menu.
3. Enter the outline you created in Review Exercise 1–1.
4. Check the outline and make any necessary corrections.
5. Save the outline with a name appropriate for your topic.
6. Close the file and exit Presentations.

LESSON 2

Working with Text Slides

OBJECTIVES

After completing this lesson, you will be able to:

1. Understand the different templates available for slides.
2. Create title and text slides.
3. Switch between different slide views.
4. Print the slides in a presentation.

Estimated Time: 1 hour

INTRODUCTION

Text slides are slides containing alphanumeric characters such as a, b, c; punctuation; and numeric characters such as 1, +, –. Text slides include title slides, bullet chart slides, data chart slides, and combinations of these types. The text for text slides is entered into text boxes that appear on the working screen. These text boxes can be supplied in predetermined positions by a *template*, or you can create and position your own text boxes.

Presentations provides eight different templates to accept different types of data for your slides. These templates include:

- None—No background, no preformatted areas for text or data.
- Background—Just the selected background; no preformatted areas.
- Title—The selected background with preformatted areas for a title and a subtitle.
- Bullet Chart—The selected background with preformatted areas for a title, a subtitle, and a bullet chart.
- Text—The selected background with preformatted areas for a title, a subtitle, and a text box.
- Org Chart—The selected background with preformatted areas for a title, a subtitle, and an organization chart.
- Data Chart—The selected background with preformatted areas for a title, a subtitle, and a data chart.
- Combination—The selected background with preformatted areas for a title, a subtitle, a bullet chart, and a data chart.

You can use each of these templates to create text slides.

CREATING A TITLE SLIDE

A *title slide* simply presents your titles and subtitles. You need an effective title to introduce your presentation. Because the title sets the tone of your work, choose it carefully—make sure it reflects the message you are trying to get across while it arouses the interest of your audience. You can also use titles as dividers between sections or main headings. No matter where you use titles, choose your words carefully and remember to use parallel grammar on all title slides.

When you begin a new slide show, the Title template is selected for you by default because Presentations assumes you will begin your presentation with a title. When you open a new slide show without making any changes in the Document Selection or New Slide Show dialog boxes, you will see the Title template screen shown in Figure 2–1.

To create a title slide:

- Double-click in the dashed box for the title and key the title text.
- Double-click in the subtitle box to insert a subtitle.

When you double-click in either of these boxes, the dashed outline changes to show a white box with a heavy blue border. This box is called the *text editor*. It contains a cursor (the blinking vertical line) that indicates where your text will begin. The box automatically changes size to contain the text you enter. When you have finished entering text, click elsewhere on the screen to close the text editor.

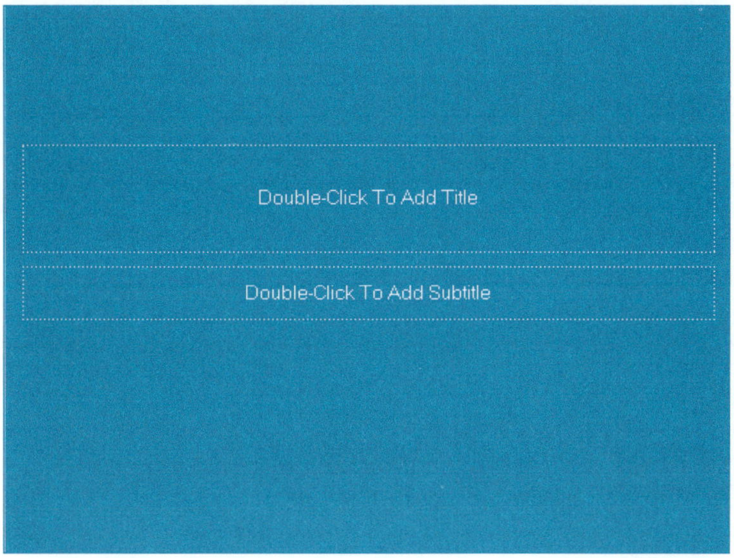

Figure 2–1
Title template screen

EXERCISE 2-1

Create a title slide for a new slide show.

1. Start Presentations and choose **OK** in the Document Selection and New Slide Show dialog boxes. The Title template screen appears.
2. Double-click in the Title box and key **ShurSweet Ice Cream.** After you have finished entering the text, click elsewhere on the screen to close the text editor box.
3. Double-click in the Subtitle box and key **Flavors of the Month.** Click elsewhere on the screen to close the text editor box.
4. Save the new slide show as **FLAVORS.**
5. Leave this slide on the screen for the next exercise.

ADDING A SLIDE

To add a slide to your slide show:

- Choose **Add Slides** from the **Slide** menu.

  or
- Click on the **Add Slides** icon in the Toolbar.

Add Slides

The Add Slides dialog box appears as shown in Figure 2–2. This dialog box allows you to choose how many slides to add and to select a template for the new slides.

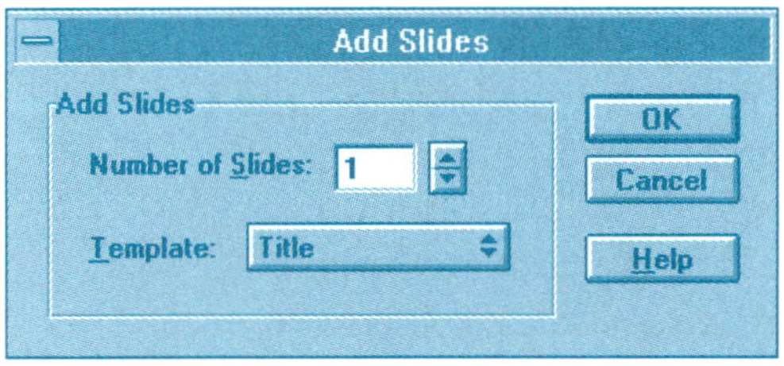

Figure 2–2
The Add Slides dialog box

▶ EXERCISE 2–2

Add a Text template slide to your presentation.

1. Select **Add Slides** from the **Slide** menu. The Add Slides dialog box appears.
2. In the Add Slides dialog box, click on the **Template** command button (it shows *Title*). Hold down the mouse button and move the pointer to *Text* to select the Text template.
3. Click **OK.** A new slide appears, with boxes for a title, subtitle, and text.
4. Leave this slide on the screen for the next exercise.

CREATING A TEXT SLIDE

To create a text slide, use the same instructions you used to create a title slide. Double-clicking on the text area opens the text editor so you can add text.

▶ EXERCISE 2–3

Add text to the new slide.

1. Double-click in the title box and key **Ice Cream Flavors**. Close the text editor.
2. Double-click in the text box and key the following entries. Press **Enter** after all but the last entry.

   Chocolate Chip
   Vanilla Bean
   Raspberry
   Mocha
3. Notice how the text box expands to accommodate each new line. Close the text editor.
4. Add another text slide and key the title **Frozen Yogurt Flavors.** Close the text editor.
5. In the text box, insert the following entries. Press **Enter** after all but the last entry.

   Milk Chocolate
   Strawberry-Banana
   Cookies 'n Cream
   Vanilla

6. Close the text editor. Save the slide show and leave this slide on the screen for the next exercise.

VIEWING THE SLIDES IN A PRESENTATION

Presentations provides several ways to view your slides as you are preparing a slide show. Four commands in the View menu give you four different ways to look at your slides.

- The *Slide Editor view* is the view that appears on your screen now. It shows the slide as it will appear when presented or printed.
- The *Outliner view* shows the slides in outline form, as you have already seen in Lesson 1.
- The *Slide List view* lists the slides in the order in which you have arranged them and gives the title of each. This view offers additional information about transitions that you will learn about later.
- The *Slide Sorter view* shows your slides as *thumbnails*, or reduced-size versions. In this view, you can easily change the slide order by simply dragging the slides.

Figure 2–3
The four slide view icons on the tool palette

You can add slides to your presentation in any of these four views by using the Add Slides command. To make it easy for you to move among these views, icons representing the four views appear on the tool palette as shown in Figure 2–3.

The Slide Select button on the Power Bar indicates which slide you are currently viewing by giving you a message such as *Slide 2 of 3*. If you click on this button, a list of the slide titles drops down. To advance to the next slide, click on the >> button to the right of the Slide Select button. To return to a previous slide, click on the << button to the left of the Slide Select button.

Slide Select

EXERCISE 2–4

Practice moving among the four slide views and add a new slide.

1. Choose **Slide List** from the **View** menu. Examine the list of three slides.
2. Choose the **Slide Sorter View** icon from the tool palette.
3. Add a slide in the Slide Sorter view:
   a. Choose **Add Slides** from the **Slide** menu.
   b. Select **Text** from the list of templates if it is not already selected. Click **OK.**
   c. A new slide, titled *Untitled,* appears in the Slide Sorter view.
4. Switch to the Slide Editor view by selecting the **Slide Editor View** icon on the tool palette.
5. Insert a title for the new slide. Key **Sherbet Flavors** and close the text editor.

6. Insert the following entries in the text box:

   Pineapple

   Orange

   Lemon

   Rainbow

7. Close the text editor and return to the Slide Sorter view.
8. Change the order of the slides:
   a. Make sure that Slide 4 is selected. (The Slide Select button will indicate *Slide 4 of 4* and the title below the slide will be highlighted.)
   b. Click anywhere on Slide 4 and hold down the mouse button as you drag to the left. The pointer changes to show a slide attached to an arrow.
   c. When a vertical rule appears to the left of Slide 3, release the mouse button. Slide 4 should now be Slide 3.
9. Save the slide show and leave the Slide Sorter view on screen for the next exercise.

DRAWING A TEXT BOX AND INSERTING TEXT

Text Objects

Hand Pointer

You might sometimes want to add a text box of your own to a slide. Use the Text Objects tool (the *A* on the tool palette) to draw a text box and add text directly to the slide. When you click on the Text Objects tool, the pointer changes to a hand holding a box.

To create a text block on your slide:

- Move the pointer to where you want your text block to start.
- Click and drag the text box to the desired size.

You can then enter text in the text editor box just as you did previously for Text template slides.

NOTE

You can only specify the width of the text block. Presentations automatically determines the depth based on the text you enter into the block.

EXERCISE 2-5

Add a text box to Slide 1.

1. Select Slide 1 and switch to the Slide Editor view.
2. Select the **Text Objects** tool (the letter *A*) from the tool palette. The pointer changes to a hand holding a box.
3. Position the pointer about 1 inch below the subtitle and even with the left end of the red bar. Hold down the mouse button and drag the box the entire width of the slide. Release the mouse button. Your screen should look like Figure 2-4.
4. In the text editor box, key your name. Close the text editor.
5. Save the slide show and leave Slide 1 on the screen for the next exercise.

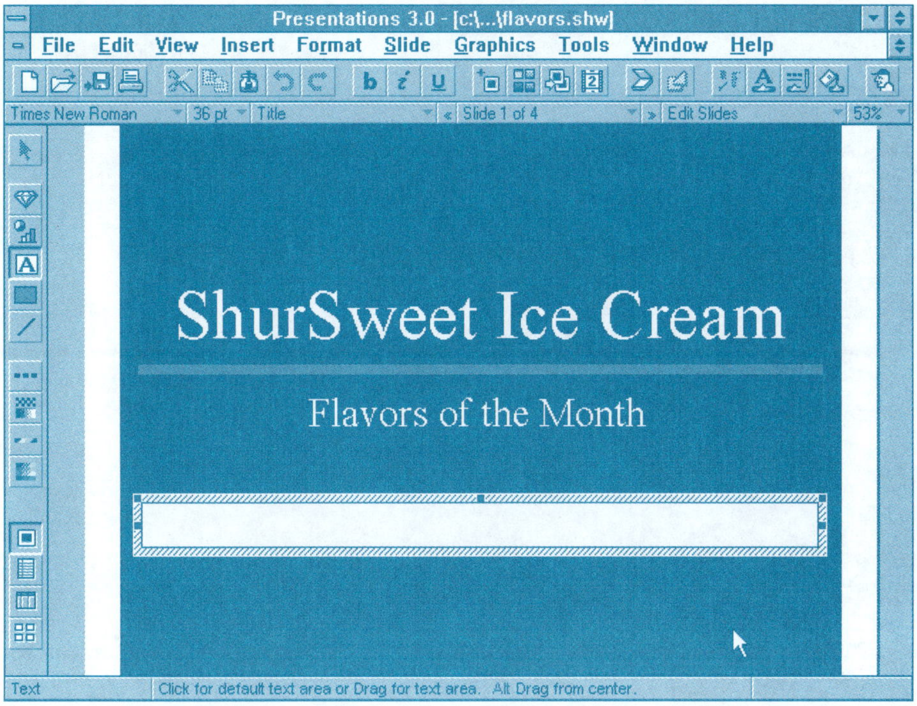

Figure 2–4
The new text box

DELETING A TEXT BOX

To delete a text box or any other object on the working screen, simply click on it to select it, then press Backspace or Delete.

PRINTING A SLIDE SHOW

When preparing your presentation, you will find it helpful to be able to print copies of your slides. Presentations gives you several printing options to do so. When you choose Print from the File menu or click the Print icon on the Toolbar, the Print dialog box shown in Figure 2–5 (on p. 32) appears. You can then select what you want to print and how many copies of it you want. You can also choose among other printing options.

Print

To choose what to print:

- Click and hold down the mouse pointer on the **Print Selection** command button.
- Choose **Slide** to print the slides one per page.
- Choose **Slide List** to print a list of the slides in the presentation.
- Choose **Handouts** to print all the slides in the presentation as thumbnails on a page.

The Output Settings area of the dialog box allows you to choose how many thumbnails per page to print. You also can choose not to print the background, and you can request that the title of each slide appear below it.

NOTE

Depending on your computer system, it can take a long time to print slides with their backgrounds. Choose the Don't Print Background check box when you need to save time.

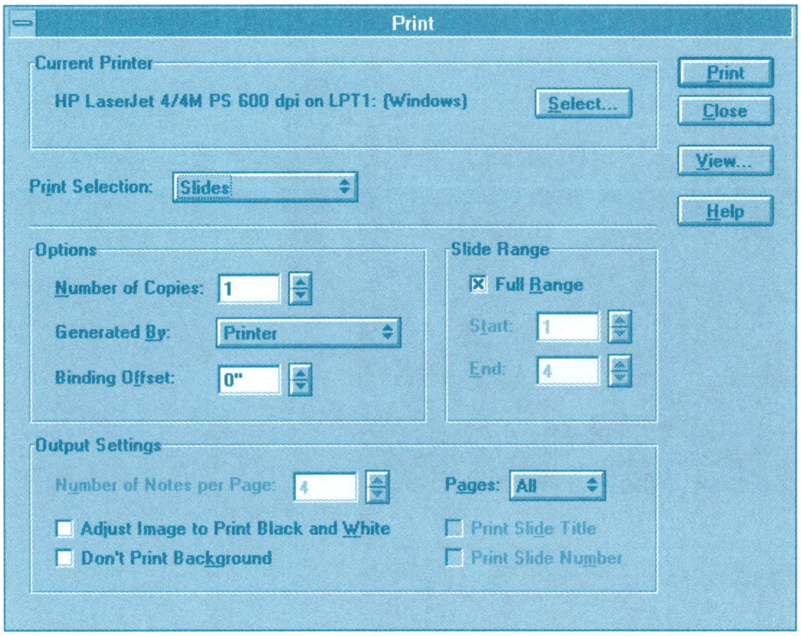

Figure 2-5
The Print dialog box

The View command button at the upper right of the dialog box allows you to see a preview of the printed output so you can make sure you have selected the options you want.

EXERCISE 2-6

Print the **FLAVORS** slide show in handout form.

1. Choose **Print** from the **File** menu. The Print dialog box appears.
2. From the Print Selection list, choose **Handouts** if it is not already selected.
3. From the Output Settings area of the dialog box, make sure Number of Slides per Page is set to 4, and click in the check box next to the Don't Print Background option.
4. Click on the **View** button to preview your handouts. When finished, click again to return to the Print dialog box.
5. Click on **Print** to print the handouts.
6. Save the slide show and exit Presentations.

ACTIVITIES

TRUE/FALSE

In the blank space before each sentence, place a **T** if the statement is true and an **F** if it is false.

______ 1. The Background template provides the selected background and two text boxes.

______ 2. The Title template is selected by default in a new slide show.

______ 3. You must enter the Slide Editor view to add new slides.

______ 4. You use the Box tool from the tool palette to draw a text box.

______ 5. You can print only thumbnail-size versions of your slides.

COMPLETION

Fill in the blank.

1. You use the ________________ to add a text box to a slide.
2. You use the ________________ view to rearrange the order of your slides.
3. The ________________ template has neither a background nor any preformatted areas for text or data.
4. The ________________, a white box with a blue border, is where you insert text.
5. The ________________ button lets you look at your work before you print it.

R E V I E W

REVIEW EXERCISE 2-1

Use the information presented below to construct a new slide show.

1. Start Presentations and begin a new slide show.
2. Change to Outliner view.
3. From the following information, create a title that expresses the message in the presentation. Use the Title and Text templates to create the slides. Adjust the titles of Slides 2–8 to conform to the guidelines given in Lesson 1 and this lesson for brevity and parallel structure. Create subtitles that enlarge on the topics expressed in the titles. Add and modify the text entries as necessary to present necessary information.

Slide 1	Title:	Create this title yourself
	Subtitle:	Your Name
Slide 2	Title:	It is important to make eye contact with audience
	Text:	Look people in the eye
		Shift eye contact from area to area
		Make eye contact with a specific person
Slide 3	Title:	Try to use gestures to add emphasis and make your presentation meaningful
	Text:	Use palm-up, open-handed gestures
		Don't let hands become focus
Slide 4	Title:	Try to model the behavior you want in audience
	Text:	For example, ask "Any questions?" and raise your hand
	Text:	Nod your head when you want agreement
Slide 5	Title:	You should use as much space as you have
	Text:	If you can, move about
		Don't pace or run
		Try reaching upward and outward to audience
Slide 6	Title:	It is a good idea to find excellent speakers to emulate
	Text:	Pay attention to body language
		Mimic their motions
		Listen to their voices

Slide 7	Title:	Always try to be enthusiastic
	Text:	Enthusiasm is contagious
		Excite your audience with your enthusiasm
Slide 8	Title:	Smile!

4. Save the presentation as **PRESENT.**
5. Print the slide show in handout form, with eight slides per page and no background.
6. Close the slide show and quit Presentations.

LESSON 3

Editing, Formatting, and Customizing Text Slides

OBJECTIVES

After completing this lesson, you will be able to:

1. Edit a text slide.
2. Move a text box.
3. Insert special characters and the date.
4. Check spelling in a slide show.
5. Change font, style, size, and appearance.
6. Select backgrounds from the Master Gallery.

Estimated Time: 1 hour

INTRODUCTION

Once you have developed your presentation, you will want to refine it to make sure your message is as clear and interesting as it can be. Presentations offers you a number of tools to make editing and formatting your text easy. You can also change the background of your slides to achieve a more interesting look with the Master Gallery.

EDITING A TEXT SLIDE

To change, delete, or add text in an existing text block, open the text editor by double-clicking on the text block. When the text editor is activated, the pointer becomes an I-beam you can use to make changes. To highlight text (select individual characters or phrases) for editing, click and drag the I-beam to highlight the appropriate text. To deselect text, click outside the selected text.

EXERCISE 3-1

Edit a text slide.

1. Start Presentations and click **OK** in the Document Selection and New Slide Show dialog boxes.
2. Open **EX3-1.SHW** from your template disk.
3. On Slide 1, double-click on the text block containing the words "Your Name." Click and drag the I-beam to highlight these words. Key your name.
4. Move to Slide 2 ("Ice Cream Flavors").
5. Double-click on the text block to open the text editor. Make the following changes to the ice cream flavors:

Change:	To:
Chocolate Chip	**Double Chocolate Chip**
Vanilla Bean	**Golden Vanilla Bean**
Raspberry	**Very Berry Raspberry**
Mocha	**Mocha Chip**

6. Save the slide show as **FLAVORS2** and leave the slide on the screen for the next exercise.

MOVING A TEXT BOX

You can easily move text boxes to new locations on the screen. Before you can move a text box, you must *select* it with the pointer.

To move a box to a new location:

- Click on the box. Eight small boxes called *handles* appear at the sides and corners of the text box, indicating that it is selected.
- With the pointer inside the text box, hold down the mouse button and drag to move the block to any position on the slide.

EXERCISE 3-2

Move a text box to a new position.

1. Go to Slide 1 and click on the text box that contains your name.
2. Hold down the mouse button as you drag the box to the bottom of the slide. A dashed line shows the outline of the text box so you can easily position it.
3. Release the mouse button. Leave this slide on the screen for the next exercise.

INSERTING SPECIAL CHARACTERS AND DATES

You can insert special information into your slides, including special characters (characters that do not appear on the keyboard) and dates.

Inserting Special Characters

You can insert characters that do not appear on the keyboard into your slides. These special characters include typographic characters (such as —, ½, ©), mathematical and scientific characters, and multinational characters (including Hebrew, Cyrillic, Japanese, and Arabic).

To insert special characters into your slides:

- Open the text editor for the text box where you want to add the character.
- Choose **Characters** from the **Insert** menu. This displays the WordPerfect Characters dialog box.
- Select the character set you want to use.
- Click on the character you want to insert.
- Click on **Insert and Close** if you want to insert only one character.

  or
- Click on **Insert** to insert the selected character and keep the dialog box open.

EXERCISE 3-3

Insert a special character into your slide.

1. Double-click on the text box containing your name at the bottom of Slide 1 to open the text editor.
2. Place the cursor after the last letter of your name and choose **Character** from the **Insert** menu.
3. Select **Typographic Symbols** from the Character Set list.

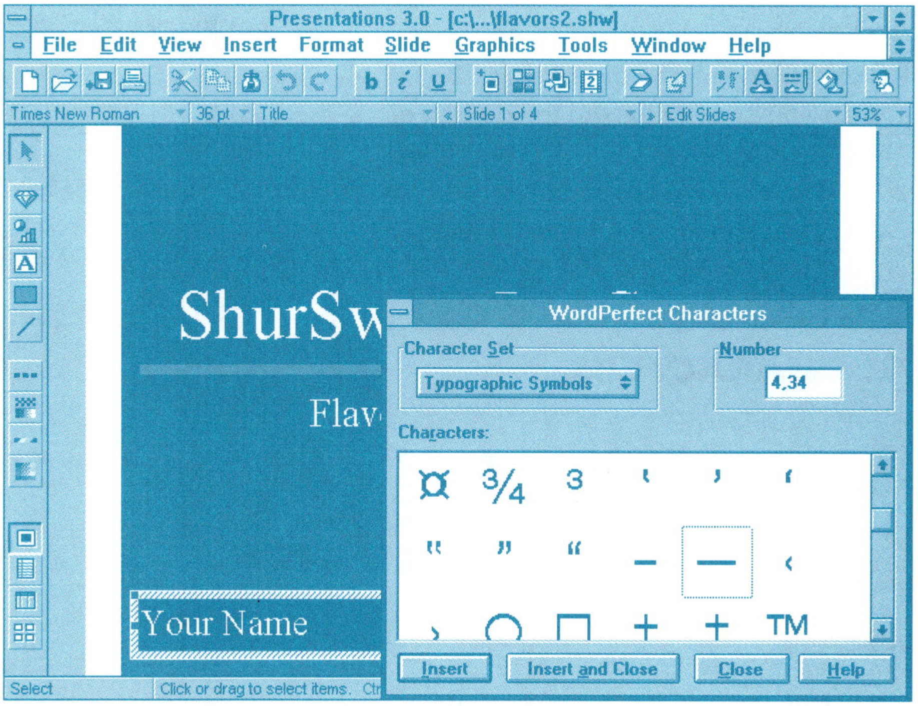

Figure 3–1
Inserting a special character

4. Click on the scroll bar until you see the dash shown in Figure 3–1. Click on the dash and choose **Insert and Close.**
5. Leave the text editor open for the next exercise.

Inserting Dates

You can also insert the current date into your document, either as text or as a code that will change to the current date each time you retrieve the document.

To insert the current date into your slide:

- Open the text editor.
- Choose **Date** from the **Insert** menu.
- Choose **Text** to insert the date as text.

  or

- Choose **Code** to insert a code for the date. A date entered as Code will change to reflect the current date whenever the file is opened.

EXERCISE 3–4

Insert the current date into the slide.

1. Choose **Date** from the **Insert** menu and select **Code** from the pop-up list to insert the date as code.
2. Save the slide show and leave it on the screen for the next exercise.

CHECKING YOUR SPELLING

Nothing is more unprofessional than spelling errors in your presentation. Presentations has a built-in spell checker to help you avoid this problem, but *you must remember* to spell check every presentation while it is still in the editing stage.

Presentations lets you build your own dictionary by adding names and terms you use frequently. When you add these words to the dictionary, the spell checker will no longer flag the words as misspelled.

You can start spell checking in any of the views of Presentations. You can check each slide separately, or you can check the entire presentation. In the Outliner, the spell check will check the entire outline. To check only part of the outline, highlight the section you want to check. In Slide Editor view, you must open the text editor for the text you want to check.

To begin your spell check:

- If necessary, select the text you want to check or open the text editor.
- Choose **Spell Check** from the **Tools** menu.

The spell check begins as soon as you select the Spell Check command from the Tools menu. When the spell checker finds a possible error, the Spell Checker dialog box appears with a list of suggested corrections, as shown in Figure 3–2. You can:

- Skip the suggestion, once or every time the highlighted word appears.
- Select a word from the list and choose **Replace.**
- Key the correct word in the Replace With box, then choose **Replace.**

NOTE

A spell checker cannot identify errors involving improperly used words, such as "Your the Boss." Proofread your work carefully!

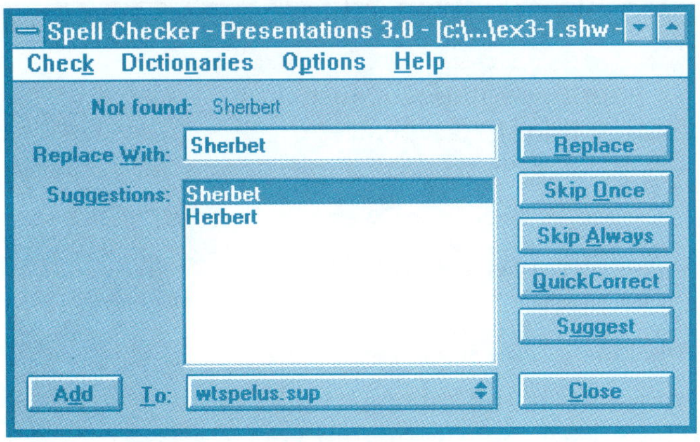

Figure 3–2
The Spell Checker dialog box

- For a repeated word, you can delete one of the words, skip the word to retain both instances, or exit the spell check by selecting **Close.**
- Continue until the document has been checked completely. To exit the spell check before it is complete, choose **Close.**

EXERCISE 3-5

Check the spelling of the current slide show.

1. Switch to Outliner view.
2. Choose **Spell Check** from the **Tools** menu.
3. The spell checker will highlight *ShurSweet* as a misspelled word. Choose **Skip Once** to ignore the word.
4. The spell checker will highlight *Sherbert.* Choose **Replace** to replace the misspelled word with the correctly spelled word *Sherbet.*
5. Correct any other errors the spell checker finds.
6. When the message box informs you that the spell check is completed, choose **Yes** to close the spell checker.
7. Save the slide show and leave it on the screen for the next exercise.

NOTE

If the Spell Checker dialog box is blocking the highlighted words, you can move it by clicking on its title bar and dragging it out of the way.

CHANGING TEXT APPEARANCE

You can change the appearance of text by selecting a specific font, style, size, pattern, color of type, or any combination of these, either before or after you create a slide. You can also change the alignment of the text—that is, how it lines up relative to the edges of the text box.

Choosing a Font

A *font* is a set of characters and numbers in one particular size and design. Each font has a name, such as Times New Roman or Arial. Presentations comes with a set of fonts that should meet most of your needs. The fonts available on your system are listed in the Font dialog box shown in Figure 3-3.

Be careful when choosing fonts for your presentation. Most designers feel that you should use no more than two typefaces on one slide.

To choose a font:

- Open the text editor and drag to select the text you want to format.
- Choose **Font** from the **Format** menu.
- In the Font dialog box, the current font is highlighted and the Sample box shows the current font and size. Select the font you want from the Font Face list.

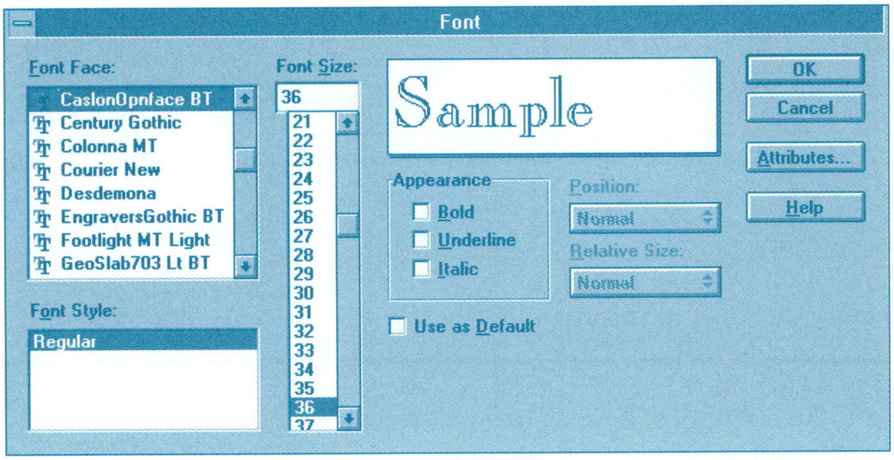

Figure 3–3
The Font dialog box

Font Selection

You can also choose a font by clicking on the Font Selection button on the Power Bar and selecting from the drop-down list. The button label changes to indicate the current font.

Choosing a Font Style

The *style* of the font refers to character enhancements such as regular, bold, italic, and bold italic. A particular font might not have all these styles available. You can see what styles are available for a font by looking at the list in the Font Style box. The current style is highlighted in the list box. You can use only one style at a time.

To choose a font style:

- Open the text editor and drag to select the text you want to style.
- Choose **Font** from the **Format** menu, and select the style from the Font Style list box.

Choosing a Font Size

Font *size* refers to the size of the characters in points. There are 72 points to 1 inch, so 12-point type is one-sixth of an inch high. The current font size is highlighted in the Font Size list. If you will be projecting your slide show, be sure that your type is large enough for viewers at the back of the room to read.

To choose a font size:

- Open the text editor and drag to select the text you want to size.
- Choose **Font** from the **Format** menu, and select the size you want to use from the Font Size list.

You can also choose a font size by clicking on the Font Sizes button on the Power Bar and selecting a size from the drop-down list. The button shows the current size.

Font Sizes

Choosing a Font Appearance

Appearance refers to character enhancements similar to font styles. The Appearance block contains three check boxes: Bold, Underline, and Italic. Use these boxes when you want to select styles *in combination* (remember, you can select only *one* style in the Font Style list box). You can check as many or as few of these styles as you wish. For example, you might want to combine bold and italic (e.g., ***this is bold italic***).

To choose a font appearance:

- Open the text editor and drag to select the text you want to format.
- Choose **Font** from the **Format** menu, and select the appearance(s) you want to use from the Appearance list.

EXERCISE 3-6

Change font, style, size, and appearance in the slide show.

1. Switch to Slide Editor view. On Slide 1, double-click on the title to open the text editor. Drag the I-beam to highlight the title text.
2. Choose **Font** from the **Format** menu to open the Font dialog box.
3. Select **Arrus BT** from the Font Face list, **Bold** from the Font Style list, and **60** from the Font Size list. After you make your selections, click on **OK**.
4. Close the text editor and observe how the title has changed in appearance.
5. Double-click on the subtitle. Using the directions in Steps 1–4, change the subtitle to **Arrus BT, Bold Italic,** and **48 points.**
6. For Slides 2–4, change titles to **Arrus BT, Bold, 48 points.** Change text to **Arrus BT, Bold Italic, 40 points.**
7. Save the slide show and leave it on the screen for the next exercise.

Changing Text Justification

Justification refers to how text lines up relative to the edge of the text box. Left-justified text aligns at the left edge of the text box. Center-justified text is aligned at the center of the text box, with equal space to the left and right edge. Right-justified text aligns at the right edge of the text box.

You cannot change the justification for the preformatted text boxes supplied with templates. However, you *can* change justification for text boxes you draw yourself. To change justification for a text box you have created:

- Double-click on the text box to open the text editor.
- Choose **Justification** from the **Format** menu. From the pop-up menu, select the desired justification.

EXERCISE 3-7

Change the justification of text in a text box.

1. Move to Slide 1 and double-click on the text box containing your name and the date.
2. Choose **Justification** from the **Format** menu. From the pop-up menu, select **Center**.
3. The text should appear centered in the text box.
4. Save the slide show and leave it on the screen for the next exercise.

Changing Text Attributes

The Text Attributes command on the Format menu lets you further customize your text. You can use the Text Attributes dialog box (Figure 3–4) to change the foreground and background colors of text, specify the fill pattern for any object, outline text in a contrasting color, and even blend colors in an object using the Gradient feature.

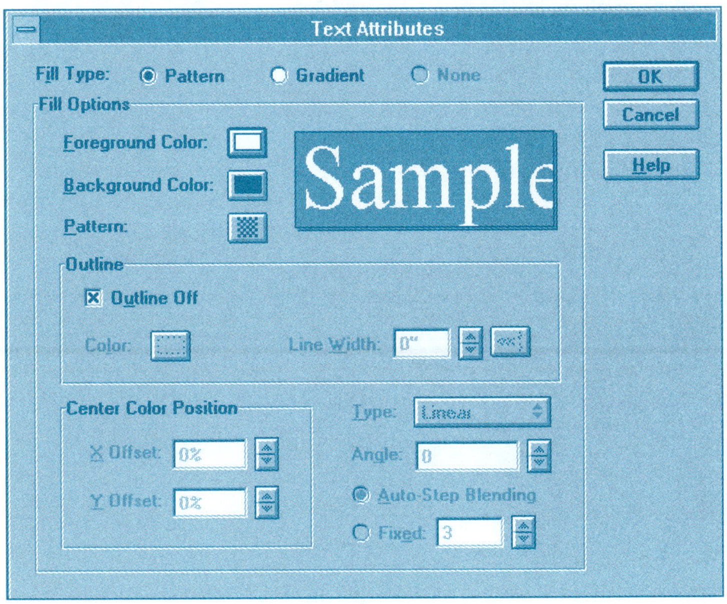

Figure 3–4
The Text Attributes dialog box

To change a text attribute:

- Select the text you want to change.
- Choose **Text Attributes** from the **Format** menu.

- To change a foreground, background, or outline color, click on the color button to the right of the option. A color grid appears. Select anywhere in the grid or click on one of the predefined colors at the top of the grid.
- Click **OK** when finished.

EXERCISE 3-8

Change text attributes.

1. Slide 1 should be on the screen. Change the color of the title text:
   a. Select the title text.
   b. Choose **Text Attributes** from the **Format** menu.
   c. Click on the box to the right of the Foreground Color option. A color grid appears.
   d. Select the light blue color at the top of the grid (fifth color box from the right). Click **OK.**
   e. Close the text editor and observe the new color of the title text.
2. Change the subtitle text to a color of your choice using the directions in Step 1.
3. Save the slide show and leave it on screen for the next exercise.

CHANGING BACKGROUNDS WITH THE MASTER GALLERY

Presentations provides a variety of backgrounds created by professional graphic designers for you to use in your slide shows. These 66 predesigned backgrounds are called *masters*. You can choose a master from the Master Gallery (Figure 3–5) before you begin a new slide show from the New Slide Show dialog box. You can also change the master at any time after you have begun a slide show.

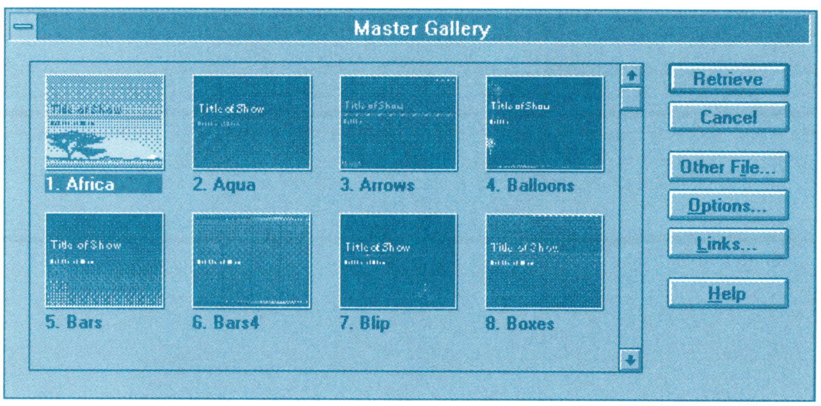

Figure 3–5
The Master Gallery dialog box

Each master gives you not only a different background, but also different options for text layout. Some masters automatically center all text, for example, while others left-justify text.

To select a master from the Master Gallery:

- For a new slide show, click on the **Gallery** button in the New Slide Show dialog box. Select the master you want to use and click on **Retrieve.**
- For an existing slide show, choose **Master Gallery** from the **Slide** menu, select the desired master, and click on **Retrieve.**

  or
- Click on the **Master Gallery** icon on the Toolbar, select the desired master, and click **Retrieve**.

EXERCISE 3-9

Change the background master for the slide show.

1. Choose **Master Gallery** from the **Slide** menu. Scroll to view all the available masters.
2. Select background number 51, **Slash**.
3. Choose **Play Slide Show** from the **Slide** menu to view your completed slide show.
4. When you have finished viewing the slides, save the slide show. Print handouts with six slides per page (print with backgrounds, if desired).
5. Close the file and exit Presentations.

A C T I V I T I E S

TRUE/FALSE

In the blank space before each sentence, place a **T** if the statement is true and an **F** if it is false.

______ 1. To edit a text block, you must open the text editor.

______ 2. The spell checker can locate all text errors in your slide show.

______ 3. You can select as many font styles as you like.

______ 4. You can choose a new background at any time after you have begun a slide show.

______ 5. You can move a text box to any position on a slide.

COMPLETION

Fill in the blank.

1. ________________ refers to character enhancements such as regular, bold, italic, and bold italic.
2. The way text lines up relative to the edge of the text box is called ________________ .
3. You use the ________________ dialog box to change text attributes.
4. You use the ________________ dialog box to change the size of the typeface.
5. To insert special characters into your slide, choose Characters from the ________________ menu.

R E V I E W

REVIEW EXERCISE 3–1

In this exercise, you will edit and format an existing slide show.

1. Start Presentations and begin a new slide show.
2. Open **REX3-1.SHW** from the template disk.
3. Open the Master Gallery and select master 31, **Ice**.
4. Change the colors of the title and subtitle on Slide 1 to colors that contrast more strongly with the background:
   a. Select the text to change and choose **Text Attributes** from the **Format** menu.
   b. Select the **Pattern** button at the top of the Text Attributes dialog box.
   c. Choose a new foreground color from the color palette.
5. Add a text box on Slide 1 and insert the date as a code. Center the date on the slide.
6. Add text boxes on Slides 2–4 and insert at least two items on each slide to serve as supporting information for the claims in the title and subtitle. Choose an appropriate font, style, and color for these entries.
7. Save the slide show as **SHUREDIT**. Print the slide show as handouts with six slides per page and no background.
8. Close the file and exit Presentations.

LESSON 4

Working with Bullet Charts and Tables

OBJECTIVES

After completing this lesson, you will be able to:

1. Create a bullet chart.
2. Change bullet styles.
3. Create a table.
4. Format data in a table.

Estimated Time: 1 hour

INTRODUCTION

In addition to adding plain text to your slides, Presentations also lets you add *text charts*. There are two types of text charts: bullet charts and data charts.

Bullets are small symbols (•, ◆, ➢, etc.) that mark the beginning of a line of text. The Bullet Chart template allows you to set up a list of bulleted items. Bullet charts assist you and the audience by clearly marking each point in a list of entries. These charts make an excellent source for you to follow when speaking, instead of using notes.

Tables are sets of data entries arranged in rows and columns. The Data Chart template allows you to create a slide with a table. When you select this template type, Presentations provides you with a spreadsheet-like guide (the *datasheet*) that enables you to easily set up columns of text and numbers.

CREATING BULLET CHARTS

You create a bullet chart the same way you create any other text slide. You can select the Bullet Chart template from the Template command button in the New Slide Show dialog box before beginning a slide show, or you can select it from the Power Bar in the Presentations working screen.

When you select the Bullet Chart template, Presentations displays a screen that looks like the Text template screen. As for a text slide, you have boxes for a title, a subtitle, and text. Each line of text that you enter, however, will be preceded by a bullet character.

EXERCISE 4-1

Create a bullet chart with a master from the Master Gallery.

1. Start Presentations and click on **OK** in the Document Selection dialog box.
2. In the New Slide Show dialog box, click on the **Gallery** command button and select master 4, **Balloons.** Click **Retrieve.**
3. Click on the **Template** command button and hold down the mouse button. Move the highlight to **Bullet Chart** and release the mouse button. Click **OK.**
4. In the title box, key **ShurSweet Announces:** and close the text editor.
5. In the subtitle box, key **Seasonal Party Favorites** and close the text editor.

6. In the text box, key the following entries. Note how each new line is preceded by a round bullet character.
   Peppermint Stick Crunch
   Cherry Vanilla
   Firecracker Cinnamon Chip
   Pumpkin Swirl
7. Close the text editor. Your screen should resemble Figure 4–1.
8. Save the new slide show as **PARTYFAV** and leave the slide show on the screen for the next exercise.

Figure 4–1
The completed bullet chart

CHANGING BULLET STYLES

Presentations allows you to customize the look of your bullet chart. Using the Define Bullets/Fonts command from the Format menu, you can change the bullet style and the font and add boxes and frames to your slides.

To customize the bullet chart:

- Click on the bullet chart to select it.
- Choose **Define Bullets/Fonts** from the **Format** menu.

The Define Bullets/Fonts dialog box appears. This box contains three option buttons for Bullets, Font, and Box/Frame. Select the button for the type of element you want to change. For bullets, you can change color, justification, and bullet type. For font, you can change the typeface, style, size, and color. For boxes/frames, you can change shape, frame, position, and fill color attributes.

EXERCISE 4–2

Change the bullet style.

1. Click on the bulleted text portion of the slide to select it.
2. Choose **Define Bullets/Fonts** from the **Format** menu. The Define Bullets/Fonts dialog box appears.
3. Click on the **Bullets** option button. The dialog box changes to show options for bullet styles and justification, as shown in Figure 4–2.

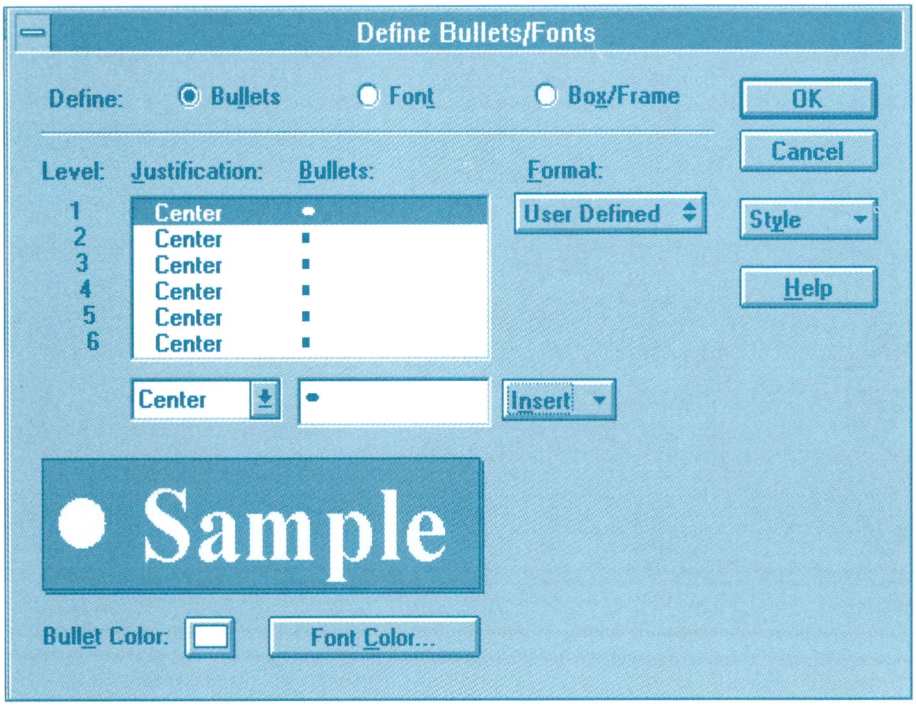

Figure 4–2
The Define Bullets/Fonts dialog box

4. Click on the first entry in the list box, which shows Center justification and a large bullet.
5. Change the bullet style:
   a. Double-click in the bullet format box, which appears to the left of the Insert command button. This should highlight the bullet displayed there. Press **Delete** to delete the bullet.
   b. Click on the **Insert** command button.
   c. From the drop-down list, select the last entry, **Small Bullet.**
   d. The Sample box changes to show the new bullet size. Click **OK.**
6. Save the slide show and print the slide as a handout, with two slides per page and no background.
7. Close the file and leave the Document Selection dialog box on the screen.

CREATING A TABLE

The Presentations Data Chart template allows you to insert tabular matter in a slide. If the table is to be the main focus of the slide, choose the Data Chart template either in the New Slide Show dialog box or from the Power Bar in the working screen. When you select this template, Presentations provides a screen like the one in Figure 4–3.

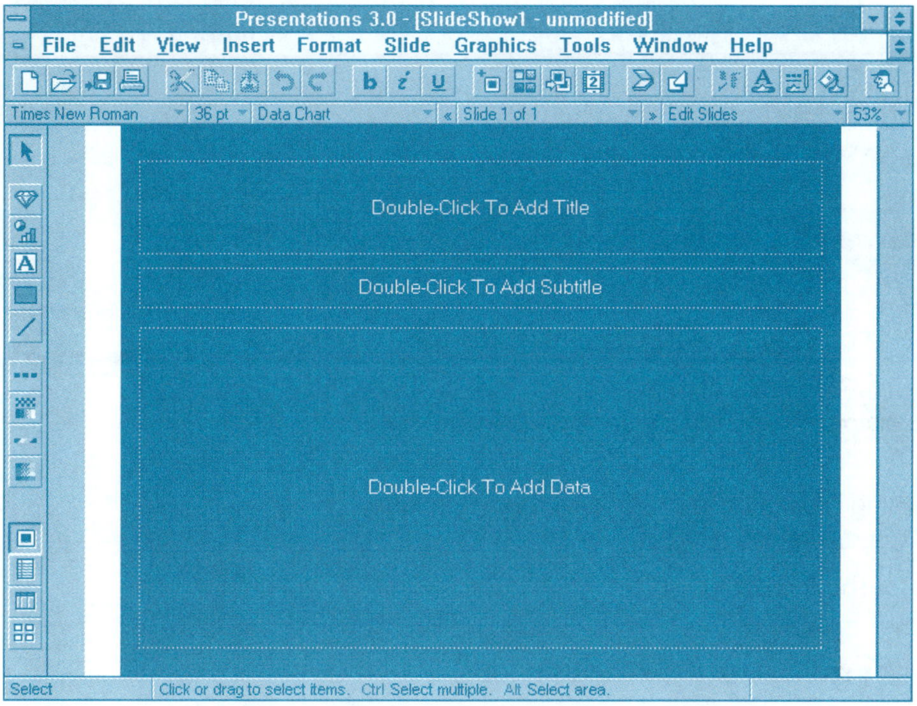

Figure 4–3
The Data Chart template screen

To add data, double-click in the rectangle labeled *Double-Click To Add Data*. This opens the chart editor, and the Data Chart dialog box appears to request information about the type of data chart you want.

You might also want to add a table to a slide that has a different template. To insert a table in a slide with a template other than Data Chart:

- Choose **Data Chart** from the **Insert** menu.

  or

- Click on the **Chart Object tool** icon on the tool palette.

Chart Object

- The pointer changes to a hand holding a box. Click and drag to create a chart block. After a few seconds, the Data Chart dialog box appears.

The Data Chart dialog box contains the chart gallery, a list of the types of charts available with small pictures of each format available for each type of chart. Select the type of data chart you want to use and click on OK. The table and a datasheet (shown in Figure 4–4) appear.

The datasheet has numbered rows and lettered columns. Each cell is represented by the column-row intersection, such as A1, B13, etc. To move around the datasheet, you can use the mouse to move the pointer, press Tab, or use the Go To Cell option in the Edit menu. When you are working in the datasheet, the pull-down menu items affect the contents of the selected cells.

NOTE

You can click and drag the edges of the datasheet to make it larger so it is easier to read.

Datasheet

	Legend	A	B	C	D
Labels		1st Qtr	2nd Qtr	3rd Qtr	4th Qtr
1	North	90	50	65	85
2	South	50	40	45	70
3	East	25	30	40	20
4	West	10	20	30	45
5					

Figure 4–4
The datasheet

EXERCISE 4–3

ShurSweet management wants you to prepare a table of their five top-selling flavors of ice cream.

1. The Document Selection dialog box should be on your screen. Click **OK.**
2. In the New Slide Show dialog box, choose the **Data Chart** template, then click **OK.** The Data Chart template screen appears.
3. Insert a title and subtitle for the slide show:

   Title: **ShurSweet Ice Cream**

   Subtitle: **Your name—Current date** (insert date as Code)
4. Double-click on the data chart block to open the Data Chart dialog box.
5. Select **Table** from the Chart Type list box.
6. Click on the first table type (the top left table in the gallery), then click **OK.**
7. The datasheet will appear, as shown in Figure 4–4.
8. Leave the datasheet on the screen for the next exercise.

Working with the Datasheet

The datasheet shows sample entries that will help you set up your table. To replace these sample entries, click on the cell where you want to enter text and begin keying. After you have finished the entry, press Enter to insert the new data.

The datasheet has four columns and four rows of sample data. If your table requires more columns and rows, enter the additional column headings in the columns labeled E, F, G, and so on. Enter additional rows of data in the rows marked 5, 6, 7, and so on.

If your table requires fewer columns or rows than shown in the sample, you must delete the sample entries, or they will appear in your table. To delete columns or rows:

- Click on the column letter or the row number to select the entire column or row.
- Choose **Delete** from the **Edit** menu. A message will ask if you wish to delete the cells in the selected column or row.
- Choose **OK** to delete the cells or **Cancel** to leave the datasheet as is.

EXERCISE 4-4

Enter the data into the datasheet.

1. Click in the cell that currently contains the text *1st Qtr.* Key **Units Sold** and press **Enter**.
2. Press **Tab** or use the Right arrow to move to the cell currently labeled *2nd Qtr.* Key **Sales Revenue** and press **Enter**.
3. Click in the cell currently labeled *North.* Key **Chocolate,** press **Tab,** key **500000,** press **Tab** again, key **845000,** and press **Enter.** Your screen should look similar to Figure 4–5.

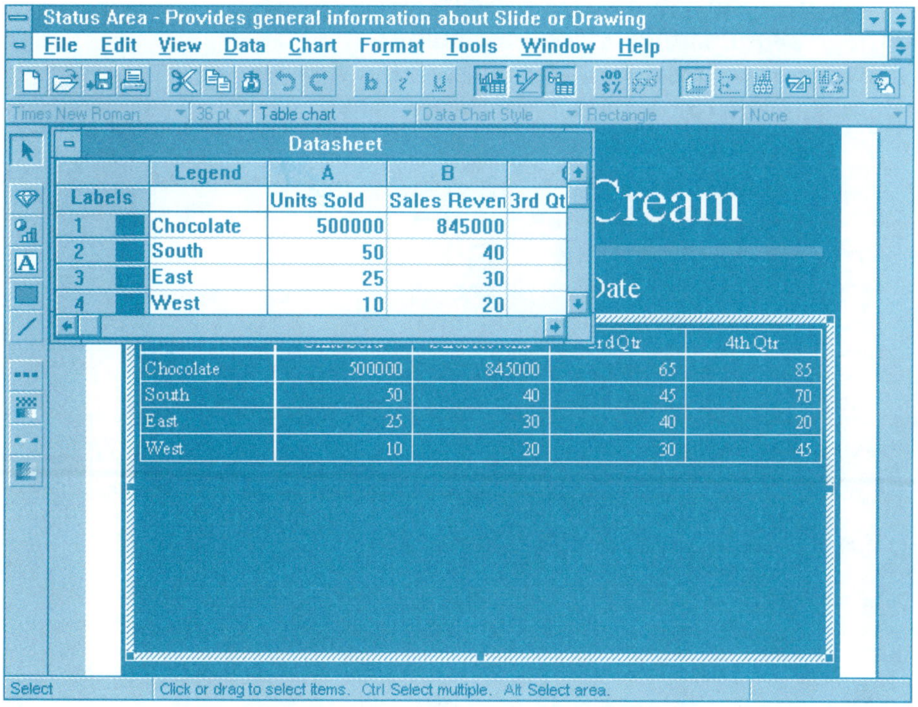

Figure 4–5
The datasheet partially filled in

4. Enter the remaining data in the datasheet, following the instructions above. Key the following information:

	Units Sold	Sales Revenue
Vanilla	**527000**	**837930**
Chocolate Chip	**450000**	**805500**

Strawberry	**420000**	**667800**
Butter Pecan	**350000**	**591500**

5. Remove the sample data shown in Columns C and D:
   a. Click on the letter *C* to select the entire column.
   b. Choose **Delete** from the **Edit** menu.
   c. When the warning message appears, click **OK** to delete the cells in the column.
   d. The data in Column D moves to the left and now appears in Column C.
   e. Delete the data in Column C.

Control Menu

6. The datasheet is now completed. Close the datasheet by double-clicking its Control menu box.
7. The slide now shows the data in place. Click outside the chart to close the chart editor.
8. Save the slide show as **TOPSELL** and leave the slide on the screen for the next exercise.

NOTE

If you see a dialog box asking whether to save the entire file or only selected items, click on Entire File, then click OK.

Formatting the Data

After you have entered the data, you can use the Format command found in the Data menu to change the format of the numeric data. The Format dialog box provides a variety of formatting options, including currency, comma separator, fixed point, decimals or no decimals, and so on (Figure 4–6). These formats are similar to those used in spreadsheets.

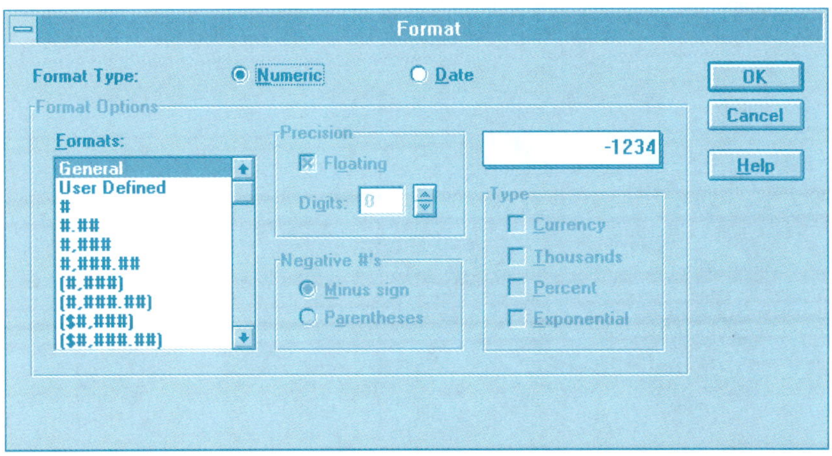

Figure 4–6
The Format dialog box

To change the format of numbers:

- Open the chart editor by double-clicking on the table, and choose **Datasheet** from the **View** menu to display the datasheet.
- In the datasheet, select the numbers you want to format by clicking on individual cells or by dragging to highlight a number of adjacent cells.

- Choose **Format** from the **Data** menu.
- Select the desired format from the Formats list box and click **OK.**

EXERCISE 4-5

Format the data in the table to show comma separators and dollar signs.

1. Open the chart editor by double-clicking on the table. Choose **Datasheet** from the **View** menu to display the datasheet.
2. Add comma separators to the values in the Units Sold column:
   a. Select the cells containing numbers in the Units Sold column by dragging from cell A1 to cell A5.
   b. Choose **Format** from the **Data** menu. The Format dialog box appears.
   c. Select **#,###** in the Formats list box and click **OK.**
3. Add comma separators and dollar signs to the values in the Sales Revenue column:
   a. Select the cells containing numbers in the Sales Revenue column by dragging from cell B1 to B5.
   b. Choose **Format** from the **Data** menu.
   c. Select **($#,###)** in the Formats list box and click **OK.**
4. Click elsewhere on the slide to close the datasheet and the chart editor.
5. Save the slide show. Print the slide in handout form, with two slides per page and no background.
6. Close the file and exit Presentations.

ACTIVITIES

TRUE/FALSE

In the blank space before each sentence, place a **T** if the statement is true and an **F** if it is false.

______ 1. You use the Text template to set up a list of bulleted items.

______ 2. You can use tables only on data chart slides.

______ 3. After you have entered the data, you can format the numbers in a variety of ways.

______ 4. You cannot change the style of bullets in a bullet chart.

______ 5. You can create a data chart only on the Data Chart template.

COMPLETION

Fill in the blank.

1. A/an ________________ is a small symbol that marks the beginning of a line of text.
2. A/an ________________ is a set of data entries arranged in columns and rows.
3. You must open the ________________ before you can modify a table.
4. To change numbers to currency or percent format, choose the ________________ command from the ________________ menu.
5. You enter data for a table or chart into the ________________ .

R E V I E W

REVIEW EXERCISE 4–1

1. Create an outline from the *Guidelines for Creating Bullet Charts* below.
2. When you are satisfied with the outline, select the templates appropriate for each slide. Format the presentation as desired with masters, fonts, and bullet styles.
3. Save the slide show as **BULLETS** and print it as a handout with no background.
4. Close the file.

Guidelines for Creating Bullet Charts

- Try not to use more than eight bullets per chart. If you have more items, you might try breaking the chart into two smaller charts.
- Build your bullet entries consistently. For example, if you begin one bullet item with a verb, begin all items with a verb; if you use one phrase for most entries, use one phrase for all entries; if you use complete sentences for most entries, make all entries complete sentences.
- Use consistent punctuation and capitalization.
- Use the same bullet style throughout your presentation.
- Try to keep items approximately the same length.
- Use strong verbs and minimize the use of prepositions.
- Use strong headings to attract attention.

REVIEW EXERCISE 4–2

All of the cities listed below are in Florida.

1. Create a data chart slide with a table that includes the city, its population in 1980, and its population in 1990. You can use a master of your choice.
2. Use an appropriate title and subtitle, and include your name.

	1980	**1990**
Belle Glade	**16177**	**16535**
Bradenton	**43769**	**30228**
Cocoa Beach	**12123**	**10926**
Daytona Beach	**61991**	**54176**
Ft. Myers	**45206**	**36638**
Gainesville	**85075**	**81371**

3. Format the data cells to include comma separators.
4. Save the slide show as **FLORIDA** and print it as a handout. Print the background if desired.
5. Close the file and exit Presentations.

LESSON 5

Using Drawing Tools and QuickArt

OBJECTIVES

After completing this lesson, you will be able to:

1. Use the drawing tools in the tool palette.
2. Create graphics for your presentations.
3. Edit graphic objects you have created.
4. Use QuickArt images.
5. Rotate and skew graphic objects.

Estimated Time: 1½ hours

INTRODUCTION

A picture is worth a thousand words. Since you know you can usually improve your slides by using fewer words, if you can use a picture and add the information of a thousand words, the important role graphics can play in your presentation becomes obvious.

You can use graphics to illustrate, set moods, and get attention. However, some of the same rules that apply to text also apply to graphics. Just as too many words can clutter slides and obscure meaning, so can too many graphics. Overuse can distract your audience, obscure your meaning, and detract from your message.

Presentations has a complete range of drawing tools to help you create sophisticated graphic images for your slides. Presentations also provides a wide array of QuickArt images (*clip art*, or predesigned graphic images) you can add to your slides.

CREATING A DRAWING

You can create a drawing on any Presentations template. Presentations offers a selection of drawing tools that allow you to draw shapes and lines of various kinds. Other commands let you change the color and pattern of objects and lines.

To access the drawing tools:

- Choose **Drawing Tools** from the **Insert** menu to view a pop-up menu list of tools.

  or

- Select drawing tools from the tool palette at the left of the drawing area.

EXERCISE 5-1

Open a file for a new drawing.

1. Start Presentations.
2. In the Document Selection dialog box, click **OK** to create a new slide show.
3. In the New Slide Show dialog box, select master 59, **White2.** Select the **Background** template and click **OK.**
4. Choose **Drawing Tools** from the **Insert** menu and leave the pop-up menu on the screen for the next exercise.

Selecting Drawing Tools

The Drawing Tools pop-up menu shown in Figure 5–1 lists the available drawing tools. Each of these drawing tools is also available on the tool palette. If you choose a drawing tool from the menu, you will see the icon representing that tool on the tool palette. These tools are briefly described in Table 5–1.

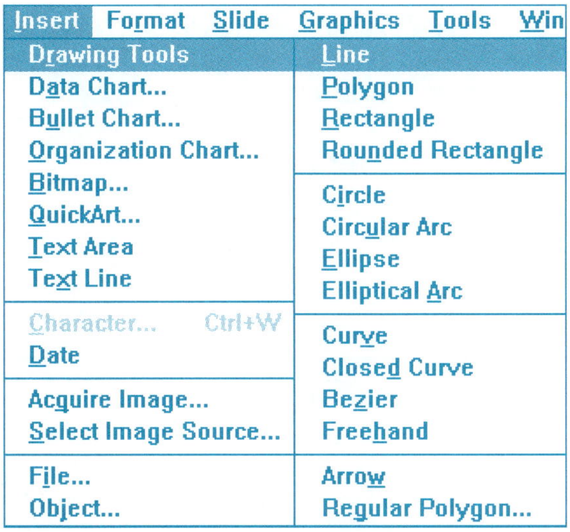

Figure 5–1
The Drawing Tools pop-up menu

Table 5–1
The Presentations drawing tools

Icon	Tool Name	Function
	Line	creates a straight line
	Polygon	creates a multisided object
	Rectangle	creates a rectangle or square
	Rounded Rectangle	creates a rectangle/square with rounded corners
	Circle	creates a circle
	Circular Arc	creates a portion of a circle
	Ellipse	creates circles and ovals
	Elliptical Arc	creates a portion of an ellipse
	Curve	creates a line with one or more rounded joints
	Closed Curve	creates a solid object with curved lines
	Bezier	creates a Bezier curve
	Freehand	creates freehand lines and drawings
	Arrow	creates an assortment of arrow shapes and sizes
	Regular Polygon	creates a multisided object with uniform sides

The drawing tools on the tool palette are organized within two icons. The Closed Object tool gives you access to squares, rectangles, circles, ellipses, polygons, and so on. The Line Object tool lets you create straight, diagonal, and curved lines of various kinds. When you click on an object tool on the tool palette, hold down the mouse button to display another set of icons from which you choose the specific type of object you want to create.

Closed Object

Line Object

To use a drawing tool:

- Select it from the menu or from the tool palette. The pointer changes to crosshairs.
- Position the crosshairs where you want to begin drawing the figure.
- As a general rule, you click to begin drawing and double-click to complete the object.

The status bar, shown in Figure 5–2, gives you specific directions for each object type. For example, Figure 5–2 shows that a Polygon has been selected and directs you to click to add points or double-click to end the drawing.

Figure 5–2
The status bar gives specific directions for drawing an object.

The status bar also indicates that you can press Shift to *constrain* an angle. Using this constraining feature, you can control aspects of each object type as you draw. For example, pressing Shift while you drag an ellipse will result in a perfect circle. Pressing Shift while using the Line tool lets you draw exactly horizontal, vertical, or 45° angle lines.

EXERCISE 5–2

Begin the drawing. Your completed drawing will resemble Figure 5–3.

1. Select **Ellipse** from the **Drawing Tools** pop-up menu.
2. The pointer changes to crosshairs. Position the crosshairs about 1 inch from the top and 3 inches from the left side and drag to form an ellipse about 1½ inches high to represent a balloon. By default, Presentations fills the ellipse with a blue color.
3. Draw two more ellipses in roughly the positions shown in Figure 5–3.
4. To draw the balloon strings:
   a. Select the **Line Object** tool from the tool palette, then select the straight line.
   b. Position the crosshairs at the bottom of one of the balloons and click to begin drawing the line.
   c. Drag the line to a point at the base of the three balloons, and double-click to stop drawing the line.
   d. Draw the other lines to join the bottom of the first line.
5. Use the Rectangle tool to draw a rectangle at the bottom of the slide as shown in Figure 5–3.
6. Save the drawing as **BALLOONS** and leave it on the screen for the next exercise.

NOTE

If you are not satisfied with a figure you have drawn, select it by clicking on it and delete it by pressing the Delete key.

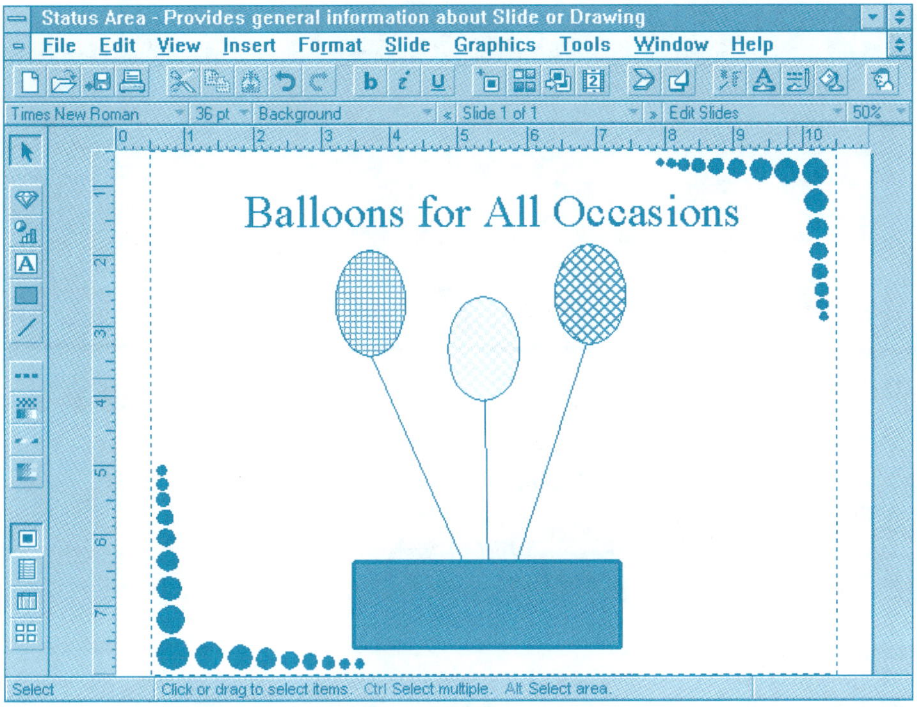

Figure 5–3
The completed drawing

Selecting and Deselecting Objects

Before you can make changes to your objects, you must select them. To select an object:

- Click on the **Select Object** tool (the pointer) from the tool palette.
- Click on the object with the pointer. Handles (small boxes) will appear around the object to indicate it is selected.
- To deselect the object, click outside the object.

Changing Line and Fill Choices

Presentations offers a wide variety of choices for line style and fill. *Line* in this case refers not only to the lines you draw with the Line tool, but also to the outlines of all the objects you draw. *Fill* refers to the pattern or color within a closed figure such as a rectangle or closed curve.

Line and fill attributes are most conveniently chosen from the tool palette. The choices are briefly described in Table 5–2 (on p. 70).

You can apply any combination of these features to any object.

To change the line or fill attribute or color:

- Select the object you want to change.
- Select the appropriate icon and hold down the mouse button to see the available choices. Move the highlight to the desired choice.

Icon	Icon Name	Function
	Line Attributes	turns line attributes on/off for drawing object
	Fill Attributes	selects fill and patterns
	Line Colors	selects color for lines and borders
	Fill Colors	selects color for fill

Table 5–2
Line and fill attributes

EXERCISE 5–3

Change the fill colors and patterns for the drawing.

1. Click on the **Select Object** icon, then select the first balloon.
2. Click on the **Fill Colors** icon on the tool palette and select red.
3. Click on the **Fill Attributes** icon and select a pattern.
4. Make the second balloon yellow with a different pattern.
5. Leave the third balloon blue, but change the pattern.
6. Select the rectangle and change the color to brown. Select the **Line Attributes** icon and choose a heavier line weight from the list at the left.
7. Save the drawing and leave it on the screen for the next exercise.

Adding Text to a Drawing

To add labels or other text to a drawing, use the Text Object tool (the letter *A*) to draw a text box. You can then insert text using the text editor and format it as you learned in Lesson 3.

EXERCISE 5–4

Add text to the drawing.

1. Select the **Text Object** tool (the *A* on the tool palette).
2. Draw a text box above the balloons the full width of the screen.
3. Key **Balloons for All Occasions** in the text box.
4. Select the text, then choose the **Font Sizes** button from the Power Bar. Choose the **48-point** size.
5. With the text still highlighted, change the justification to **Center.**
6. Save the drawing and leave it on the screen for the next exercise.

EDITING A DRAWING

Presentations allows you to change drawings in a number of ways, including resizing objects, moving them, and deleting them.

To resize an object and retain the same proportions:

- Select the object.
- Click and drag on a corner handle (dragging an inside handle stretches the object horizontally or vertically).

To move an object:

- Select the object.
- Click inside the object.
- Drag the object to its new location.

To delete an object you have already drawn:

- Select the object.
- Choose **Delete** from the **Edit** menu.

To *undelete* (replace) the last object you deleted:

- Choose **Undo** from the **Edit** menu (Presentations remembers the last ten deletions made in a current work session).

To group objects together so they can be moved or sized as a single unit:

- Click on the first object.
- Hold down the **Shift** key and click on additional objects.
- Choose **Group** from the **Graphics** menu.

EXERCISE 5–5

Edit the drawing.

1. Increase the size of the rectangle:
   a. Select the rectangle by clicking on it with the pointer tool.
   b. Drag the top right corner upward to increase the width of the rectangle by about one-half inch.
2. The rectangle is no longer centered under the balloons. Recenter it:
   a. Select the rectangle if necessary.
   b. Place the pointer within the object, click, and hold down the mouse button while you drag the rectangle to the left. An outline shows the new position of the object as you move it.
   c. When you are satisfied with the new location, release the mouse button.
3. Move the balloons closer together, and adjust the position of the strings by clicking on each object and moving it.
4. Save the drawing and print it as a handout with two slides per page. Print the background.
5. Close the file and leave the Document Selection dialog box on the screen.

ADDING QUICKART TO YOUR SLIDES

The Presentations QuickArt Gallery groups preformatted graphics into 22 main categories (Figure 5–4 on p. 72). Each category contains at least 40 different images you can incorporate into your work. You can edit, modify, rotate, skew, color, or otherwise change the QuickArt as you like.

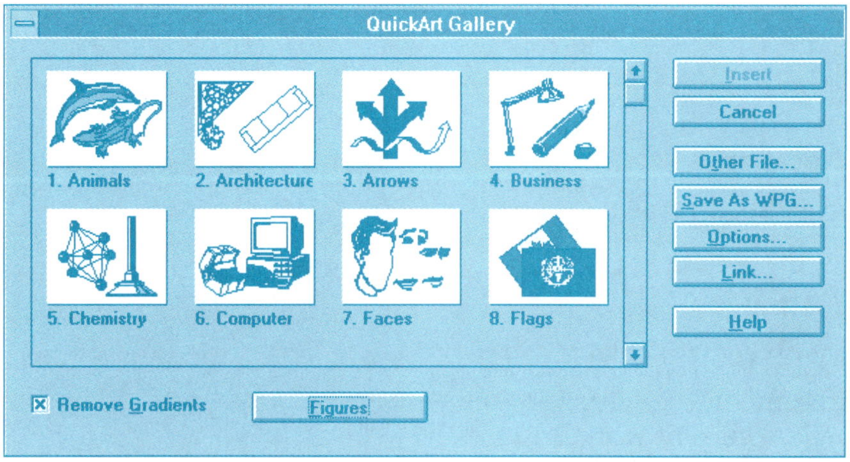

Figure 5–4
The QuickArt Gallery

You can use many of the skills you have learned for using the drawing tools with QuickArt images as well. You can change line and fill attributes as you do for an object you draw with a drawing tool. You select, move, and resize a QuickArt image the same way you do a drawn object.

However, QuickArt images also give you some other options. You can combine images to make up a new drawing, and you can edit parts of an image to customize it for your slide show.

Inserting a QuickArt Image

To insert a QuickArt image in a slide:

- On the Presentations working screen, choose **QuickArt** from the **Insert** menu.

  or

Bitmap/ Figure

- Choose the **Bitmap/Figure** tool from the tool palette.
- The pointer changes to a hand holding a box. Drag to create a box the size you want your image to be. When you release the mouse button, the QuickArt Gallery dialog box appears.
- Choose a category (scroll to see all the choices) and click the **Figures** button to open a gallery of related images.
- Select the image you want to insert and click on **Insert**.

EXERCISE 5–6

Insert a QuickArt image in a new slide show.

1. The Document Selection dialog box is on your screen. Select **Create a New Slide Show** and click **OK.**
2. In the New Slide Show dialog box, select the **Background** template from the Template list.

3. Choose **QuickArt** from the **Insert** menu. When the pointer changes to a hand holding a box, click and drag a box that is about 6 inches by 5 inches. When you finish drawing the box, the QuickArt gallery appears.
4. Select category 20, **Sports,** and click on the **Figures** button.
5. Select figure 24, **Riding,** and click on the **Insert** button. A drawing of a bicycle rider will appear in your document. Click on the pointer tool in the tool palette.
6. Save the slide show as **BIKER** and leave the slide on the screen for the next exercise.

NOTE

You can select Ruler from the View menu to activate rulers at the top and left sides of the slide. You can use these rulers to place images more accurately.

Editing a QuickArt Image

To edit a QuickArt image, use the techniques described earlier in this lesson to resize, move, and delete objects. You can also edit components of a QuickArt image by double-clicking on the image to open the *figure editor*. In the figure editor, you can click on any piece of the image to select it. This feature lets you change or even delete parts of the figure while leaving other parts intact. To select more than one part at the same time, hold down the Ctrl key while clicking on the parts you want to select.

EXERCISE 5-7

Edit the QuickArt image.

1. Double-click on the graphic to open the figure editor.
2. Click on the top of the helmet. Use the Fill Color palette to change the color.
3. Click on the bottom portion of the biker's helmet and change the color.
4. Select the body, the sleeve, and the sleeve band of the biker's jersey by holding down the **Ctrl** key while clicking on each part. Change the jersey color.
5. Save the slide show and print it as a handout with no background.
6. Close the file and leave the Document Selection dialog box on the screen.

NOTE

You might need to practice selecting parts of the image before you can easily select the piece you want. To be sure you have the desired piece, move it slightly to observe its outline.

ROTATING OR SKEWING AN OBJECT

Presentations also lets you rotate or skew an object. *Rotating* means turning the object from its original position around an invisible axis in the center of the object. *Skewing* means distorting the graphic so it appears slanted. You can rotate and skew both drawn objects and QuickArt images.

To rotate or skew an object:

- Select the object and choose **Rotate** from the **Edit** menu. The rotate and skew handles shown in Figure 5–5 will appear.
- Click on the appropriate handle and drag.

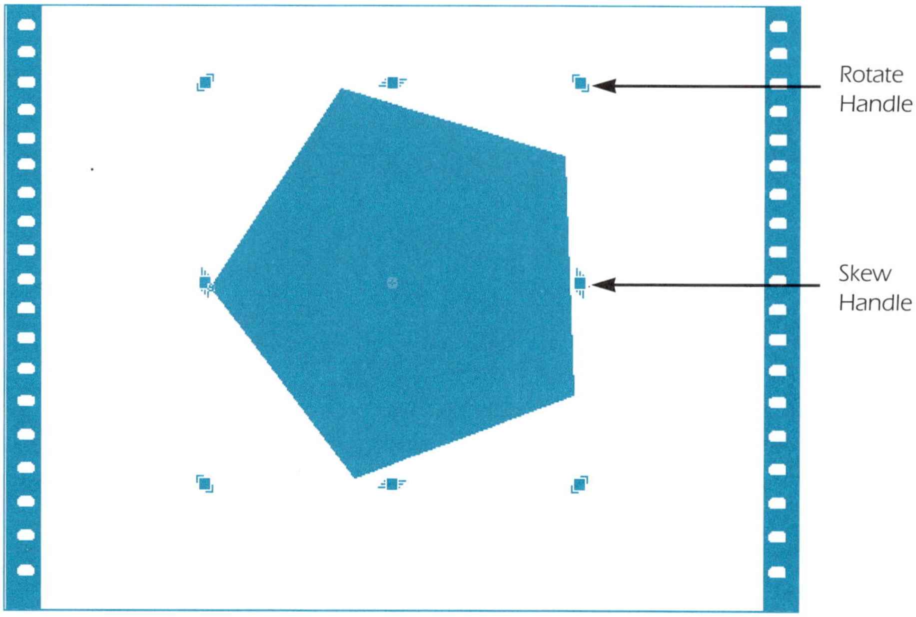

Figure 5–5
Rotate and skew handles

EXERCISE 5–8

Rotate and skew an image.

1. Retrieve **EX5-8.SHW** from the template disk. Retrieve master 66, **Zigzag.**
2. Click on the graphic, then choose **Rotate** from the **Edit** menu.
3. Rotate the graphic slightly to give the impression the biker is traveling uphill:
   a. Click on the top right corner box and hold the mouse button down.
   b. Drag the pointer to the left. The graphic rotates in the same direction.
   c. When you are satisfied with the angle of rotation, release the mouse button.
4. Now skew the graphic to give the impression of speed:
   a. Click on the skew handle at the top center of the image and hold the mouse button down.
   b. Drag the pointer to the right. The graphic outline changes to reflect the skew.
   c. When you are satisfied with the skew, release the mouse button.
5. Save the graphic as **SKEWBIKE.** Print it as a handout, with the background.
6. Close the file and exit Presentations.

ACTIVITIES

TRUE/FALSE

In the blank space before each sentence, place a **T** if the statement is true and an **F** if it is false.

______ 1. You can access the drawing tools through tool palette icons and through the Insert menu.

______ 2. You can use the Shift key with the ellipse tool to draw a perfect circle.

______ 3. To stop drawing an angle, curve, line, or freehand drawing, you click on the pointer in the tool palette.

______ 4. If you delete an object by mistake, the only way to recover it is to redraw it.

______ 5. Fill attributes apply only to solid objects, not to lines or text.

COMPLETION

Fill in the blank.

1. The ________________ lets you select each piece of a QuickArt image.
2. To use predesigned "clip art" in your slides, select ________________ from the Insert menu.
3. You select an object by ________________ .
4. You deselect an object by ________________ .
5. Distorting a figure so it appears slanted is called ________________ .

R E V I E W

REVIEW EXERCISE 5–1

Add drawings to an existing slide show.

1. Begin a new slide show by opening **REX5-1.SHW** from your template disk.
2. On Slide 1, use the Polygon and Ellipse tools to draw an ice cream cone with a scoop of ice cream.
    a. Choose appropriate colors and/or patterns for the cone and the ice cream.
    b. Group the cone and the ice cream and position them in the center of the slide.
3. On Slide 2, add an arrow to point out a new flavor.
    a. Click on the **Closed Object** icon on the tool palette and select the arrow.
    b. Draw an arrow pointing to the second flavor in the list. (*Hint:* The status bar will give you instructions for how to begin and end the arrow.) Choose a fill color for the arrow, and adjust its size and position as desired.
    c. When the arrow is completed, add a text box with the words **New Flavor!** to accompany the arrow. Choose a color for the text.
4. Save the slide show as **SHURDRAW.** Print as a handout with no background.
5. Close the file.

REVIEW EXERCISE 5-2

Add QuickArt images to an existing slide show.

1. Begin a new slide show by opening **REX5-2.SHW** from your template disk.
2. On Slide 1, insert your name and the date code in the text block that currently reads "Your name — Current Date."
3. Advance to Slide 2. Insert a QuickArt image:
   a. In the QuickArt Gallery, select category 7, **Faces.**
   b. Select image 18, **EYESF6.**
   c. Place the graphic appropriately on the slide.
4. Advance to Slide 4. Insert **HAND02** from category 12, **Hand Signs.**
5. Click on the object and select **Rotate** from the **Edit** menu. Rotate the graphic so the hand points up.
6. Advance to Slide 8 and insert QuickArt images to represent a smiling face.
   a. First, select a face from category 7, **Faces.**
   b. Use the Bitmap/Figure tool to draw a box on the face where its eyes should be. Select eyes from the Faces category.
   c. Draw boxes for a nose and mouth and select each feature from the Faces category. Make sure the mouth is smiling.
   d. Adjust all features on the face until they are the correct size and position.
7. Group all the features and the face if necessary to center the face in the slide.
8. Save the document as **FACE.** Print the slide show as a handout with eight slides per page and no background.
9. Close the file and exit Presentations.

LESSON 6

Presenting Statistics with Charts

OBJECTIVES

After completing this lesson, you will be able to:

1. Identify the different charts available in Presentations.
2. Create a statistical chart.
3. Edit a chart with the chart editor.

Estimated Time: 1 hour

INTRODUCTION

In the business world, converting information into charts and graphs and interpreting information from charts and graphs is an essential part of almost any job. These statistical representations are particularly important because they present a lot of information to the viewer in a limited space.

Because charts and graphs send such a powerful message, you must be certain they provide accurate information. Without knowing it, you can deceive your audience by unintentionally distorting the data. For example, the order in which you present data or the way you group your data might overemphasize or underemphasize certain data.

When you use statistics in your visuals, you must always be aware of the danger of distortion. Avoid using visuals that do not accurately convey the message, that mislead, or that show insignificant statistics. Try to use only visuals that emphasize or illustrate your main ideas.

TYPES OF STATISTICAL CHARTS

The types of statistical charts available in Presentations include pie charts, XY charts, and organization charts.

- A *pie chart* represents an entire group of data as a circle divided into proportional sections based on percentages of the whole. Figure 6–1 shows a pie chart.
- An *XY chart* uses a grid with horizontal (X) and vertical (Y) axes to determine placement of the data points. XY charts include bar charts, line charts, scatter charts, and area charts. While the appearance of each of these types of charts is different, they all use the X- and Y-axes to determine the placement of their data points. Figure 6–2 shows a vertical bar chart.

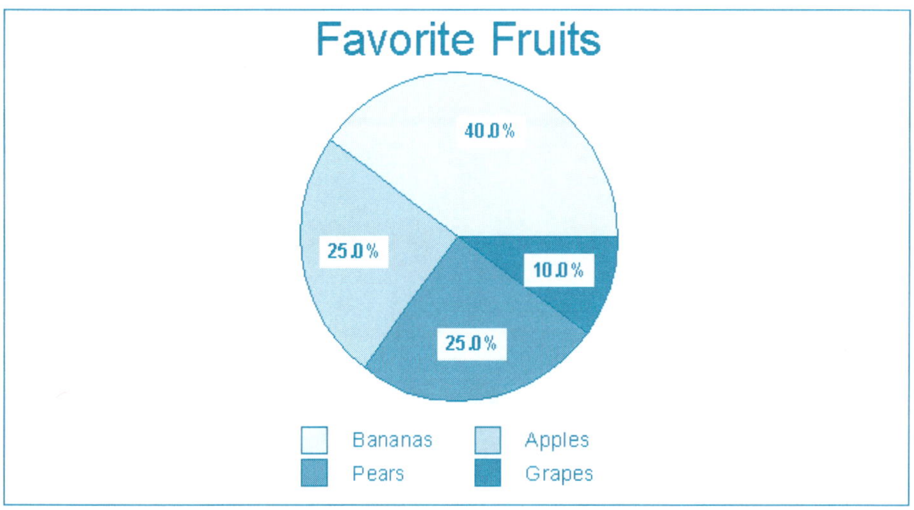

Figure 6–1
Pie chart

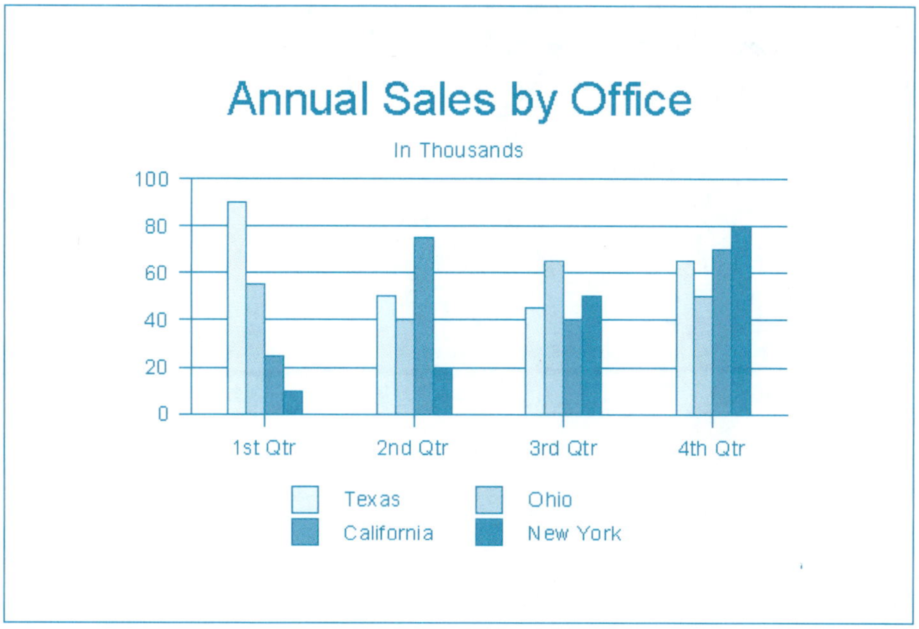

Figure 6–2
Vertical bar chart

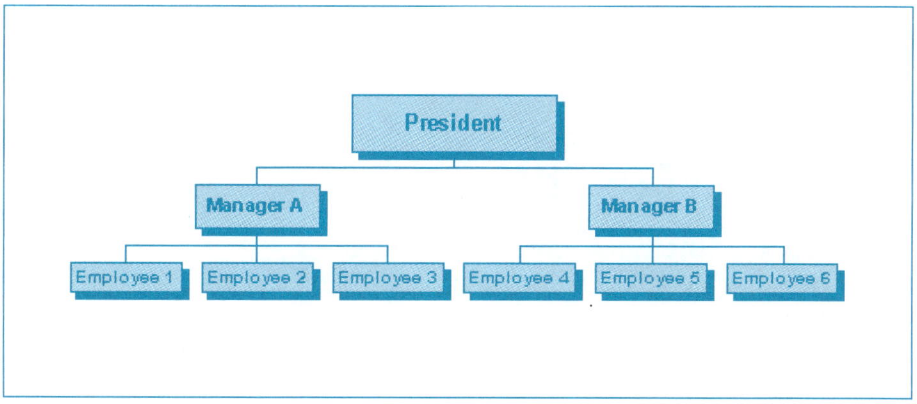

Figure 6–3
Organization chart

- An *organization chart* (Figure 6–3) indicates the relationship of individuals in an organization.

How do you decide which of these chart types to use in a given situation? Table 6–1 (on p. 82) lists the specific types of charts available in Presentations, along with a brief description of each to help you decide which is appropriate for your needs.

CREATING A STATISTICAL CHART

Your chart starts with a message. Once you have determined what your message is and what your chart will say, you can choose your chart form. How you enhance your chart is up to you, but make sure your chart conveys your message clearly. If you select a chart form and find that the data representation would be better in a different form, Presentations makes it easy to switch to another type of chart.

Table 6–1
Gallery of charts in Presentations

Use chart . . .	. . . when you want to:
Bullet	convey textual information in lists
Table	list data in columns and rows
Organization	show hierarchical relationships in an organization
Pie	show proportions and relationships of parts to the whole
Bar	show variations between components, but not in relation to the whole
Line	show trends and rate of change over time
Area	show trends and amount of change over time
Surface	show three-dimensional representations of data, with connected data points forming a surface
Scatter	show intersection points between X and Y values
Hi-Lo	show high, low, open, and close quotes for stocks

Inserting the Statistical Chart into a Slide

To insert a statistical chart into a slide:

- Choose the **Data Chart** template in the New Slide Show dialog box or from the Power Bar, then double-click in the data area to open the Data Chart dialog box.

  or

- Choose **Data Chart** from the **Insert** menu or select the **Chart Object tool** icon on the tool palette. Use the hand pointer to click once on the screen and add a full-page chart, or to drag and draw a chart box of the desired size. The Data Chart dialog box appears.

Chart Object

The Data Chart dialog box lets you choose any type of chart you want from the list box at the left side of the dialog box. Each type of chart has a gallery of available styles. Simply click the format you want to use, then click OK.

For your first statistical chart, you will create one of the most common types of statistical charts: a *bar chart*. A bar chart is particularly good for comparing quantities. For example, if ShurSweet adds a new flavor to its product line, the marketing department might want to find out how well the new flavor is selling compared to flavors already in the product line and similar flavors offered by other vendors. A bar chart can graphically illustrate these differences.

Create a bar chart.

EXERCISE 6-1

1. Start Presentations. Select **Create a New Slide Show** in the Document Selection dialog box.
2. In the New Slide Show dialog box, select a master of your choice from the Master Gallery. Choose the **Background** template.
3. Choose **Data Chart** from the **Insert** menu. The pointer changes to a hand holding a box.
4. Click on the working screen. The Data Chart dialog box appears.
5. In the Chart Type list box, select **Bar (Vert).**
6. Highlight the first chart in the top row of example bar charts and click **OK.** The datasheet appears, as shown in Figure 6–4.
7. Leave the datasheet on the screen for the next exercise.

NOTE

Make sure the Use Sample Data and 3-D check boxes are **not** selected in the Data Chart dialog box.

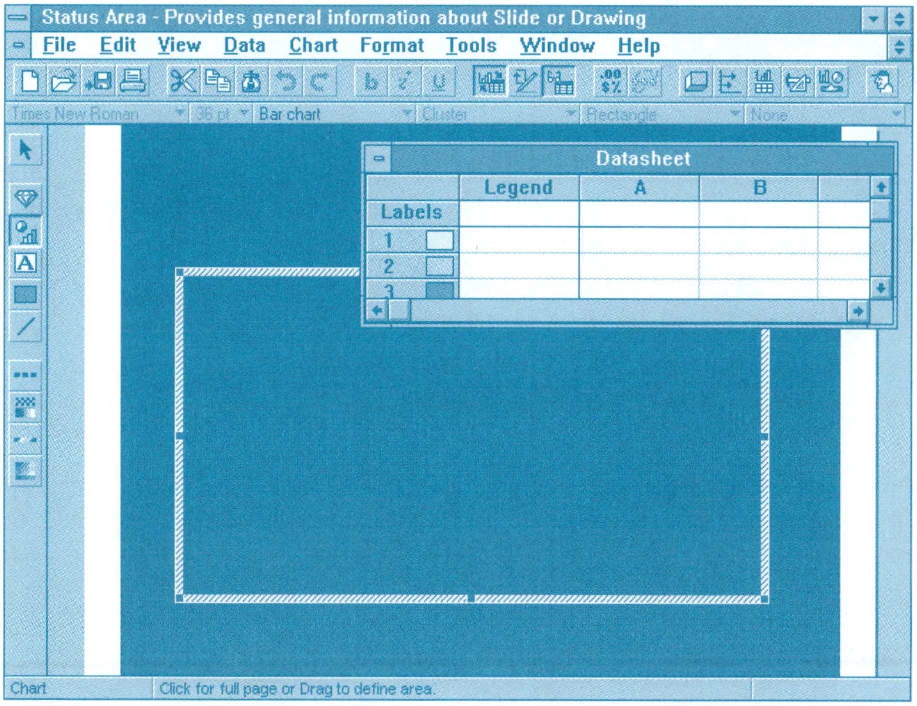

Figure 6–4
The datasheet for the new bar chart

Entering the Data

When you enter data into your chart, you should consider what aspects of the data you want to emphasize. If you want to stress the highest values, arrange the data in *descending order*, from highest to lowest. If you want to stress the lowest values, arrange the data in *ascending order*, from lowest to highest. If you want to compare data for a specific city to data for all cities in the same general geographic area, you might show the data for that city first, followed by the data for the other cities. Study your data so you can *decide which arrangement best suits the objectives of your presentation.*

As for a text chart (a table), you enter your data directly into the datasheet that appears on the screen when you choose a chart type. The datasheet now on your screen differs somewhat from the one you worked with in Lesson 4. First, note that the datasheet does not contain sample data. Next, note the Legend column and the Labels row, shown in Figure 6–5.

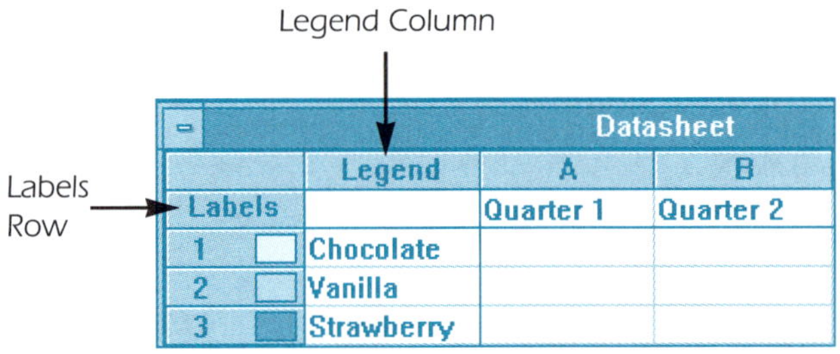

Figure 6–5
The Legend column and Labels row labeled on the datasheet

Entries that you make in the Legend column, such as *Chocolate,* will appear at the bottom of your chart as the *legend.* The color box next to each entry in this column indicates what color that bar will be on the chart. Entries that you make in the Labels row, such as *Quarter 1,* become the labels for the data in the columns below them.

EXERCISE 6–2

Enter the data and view the chart.

1. Enter the following data into the datasheet. Begin the label entries (Quarter 1) in Column A. Begin the legend entries (Chocolate) in Row 1.

	Quarter 1	**Quarter 2**	**Quarter 3**	**Quarter 4**
Chocolate	**105**	**110**	**98**	**101**
Vanilla	**125**	**99**	**110**	**122**
Strawberry	**90**	**75**	**60**	**80**

2. As you insert data, you will be able to see Presentations placing it in the new chart below the datasheet.
3. When you have finished entering the data, close the chart editor. Your new chart appears on the slide.
4. Save the slide show as **QTRSALES** and leave it on the screen for the next exercise.

NOTE

Remember that you can move and resize the datasheet as needed to make data entry easier.

Adding a Title

The title of your chart should describe what your data shows. You want your viewers to get a clear message, so use a title that will catch their attention. Be sure to use an accurate description in the title.

To add a title to your chart:

- Open the chart editor by double-clicking on the chart. Select the pointer tool from the tool palette if necessary.

- Double-click anywhere on the words *Title of Chart* to open the Titles dialog box.
- In the Titles dialog box, key the chart title and, if desired, the subtitle.
- Click the **Preview** command button to preview the title (move the Titles dialog box to see the chart title if necessary).

EXERCISE 6-3

Add a title to the chart.

1. Open the chart editor and select the pointer tool if necessary.
2. Double-click *Title of Chart* to open the Titles dialog box.
3. Key the title **Ice Cream Sales by Quarter** and click **OK.**
4. To exit the chart editor, click anywhere outside of the chart.
5. Save the slide show and print it as a handout with two slides per page and no background.
6. Close the file and leave the Document Selection dialog box on the screen.

EDITING A STATISTICAL CHART

Some editing features that you have already learned can also be used to edit statistical charts. Presentations also offers other editing features for charts that can be used for any chart type.

Moving and Resizing a Chart

Moving and resizing are the same for charts as for any other object. To move or resize a chart:

- Select the pointer tool from the tool palette.
- Click the chart to select it (handles will show around the edges of the chart).
- To move the chart, place the pointer inside the selected chart and drag the chart to the new position.
- To resize the chart, place the pointer on one of the handles and drag. Dragging a corner handle changes both height and width at the same time.

Changing the Chart Type

Once you have created a chart, you can easily change it to another chart type without having to re-enter data. You can also change the chart from two-dimensional to three-dimensional with a click of the mouse.

To change the chart type:

- Double-click the chart to open the chart editor.
- Choose **Gallery** from the **Chart** menu.
- Select the desired chart type.
- To make the chart three-dimensional, click the **3-D** check box at the bottom of the Data Chart dialog box.

EXERCISE 6-4

Resize the vertical bar chart and change it to a three-dimensional horizontal bar chart.

1. Begin a new slide show and retrieve **EX6-4.SHW** from the template disk.
2. Resize the chart to fill the screen:
   a. Click the pointer tool on the tool palette and select the chart.
   b. Click the top right corner handle and drag to increase the chart's height and width.
   c. Reposition the chart to center it and increase the size again.
   d. Continue moving and resizing until the chart handles are close to the edges of the slide.
3. Double-click the chart to enter the chart editor.
4. Choose **Gallery** from the **Chart** menu. In the Chart Type list, choose **Bar (Horz)** and select the first chart type in the top row if necessary.
5. Click the **3-D** check box at the bottom of the dialog box. Click **OK.**
6. Save the slide show as **QTRSALE2** and leave it on the screen for the next exercise.

Editing the Legend and the Title

You edit the elements of a chart (chart title, legend, labels, and so on) in the same way for all types of charts. To edit a chart element, double-click the chart to access the chart editor, then double-click the element you want to edit. Presentations then opens a dialog box that allows you to make a number of changes to the element.

EXERCISE 6-5

Edit the chart title and change the colors of the bars.

1. Double-click the chart to open the chart editor.
2. Edit the title:
   a. Double-click the title to open the Titles dialog box.
   b. Click the **Options** button at the right of the dialog box. The Titles Options dialog box appears, as shown in Figure 6-6.
   c. In the Titles Options dialog box, click the **Font** button to open the Font dialog box.
   d. Choose **Bold** Font Style and a Font Size of **54**. Click **OK** *three* times to return to the chart editor.

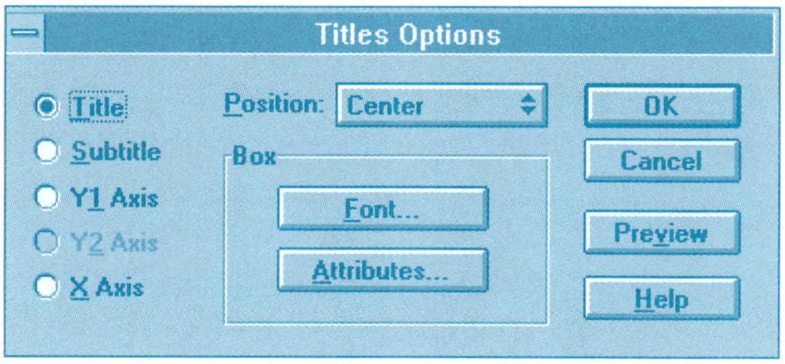

Figure 6–6
The Titles Options dialog box

3. Change the colors of the bars in the chart and legend:
   a. Double-click any of the red bars in the chart. The Series Options dialog box opens.
   b. Click the box to the right of the Color option. Choose a pink color to represent Strawberry.
   c. Click **OK** to return to the chart editor.
   d. Using the same procedure, choose appropriate colors for the Vanilla and Chocolate bars.
4. Save the slide show and print it as a handout with two slides per page and no background.
5. Close the file and exit Presentations.

ACTIVITIES

TRUE/FALSE

In the blank space before each sentence, place a **T** if the statement is true and an **F** if it is false.

_____ 1. The order in which you present data can affect how your audience interprets it.

_____ 2. A bar chart shows variations between components in relation to the whole.

_____ 3. If you want to stress the highest values in the data you are presenting, arrange your data in descending order.

_____ 4. An organization chart shows the relationship of parts to the whole.

_____ 5. Once you create a chart and enter data, you must start over if you want to change to a different chart type.

COMPLETION

Fill in the blank.

1. ________________ charts include analyses of data that produce graphic output.
2. The ________________ dialog box lets you choose a chart type from a list.
3. ________________ charts use a grid with horizontal and vertical axes to determine placement of data points.
4. A/an ________________ chart shows trends and rate of change over time.
5. Entries that you make in the ________________ column of the datasheet appear at the bottom of the chart.

REVIEW

REVIEW EXERCISE 6-1

The ShurSweet Ice Cream Company is preparing its annual report. **REX6-1.SHW** contains the first few slides of a slide show the ShurSweet management plans to present to their stockholders. In this exercise and in the next several lessons, you will add slides to this slide show to provide important data for the annual report.

The ShurSweet management wants to add a slide comparing the costs of doing business at the company's three plants.

1. Start Presentations and retrieve **REX6-1.SHW** from your template disk. This slide show contains a number of title slides indicating the main sections of the report.
2. Add a slide following the Operating Costs title slide. Use the Background template. You can switch to the Slide Sorter view to make sure you have added the new slide in the proper location.
3. Create a vertical bar chart on the new slide using the data below:

	Pittsburgh	**Roanoke**	**Gainesville**
Supplies	**40750**	**25150**	**30300**
Dairy Products	**145320**	**160100**	**200050**
Salaries	**295400**	**220840**	**180480**
Rent/Utilities	**52450**	**40110**	**33090**
Other	**22450**	**10450**	**13550**

4. Format the numbers in the datasheet to show comma separators.
5. Double-click the chart title to open the Titles dialog box and click the **Title** display check box to remove the title from the chart.
6. Rent/Utilities costs are high in Pittsburgh because of outdated facilities. New premises are being constructed that will lower these costs. Dairy Product costs are unusually high in Gainesville. The Gainesville manager is seeking new dairy suppliers to lower costs. Add a bullet chart below the bar chart to explain the costs and how the managers plan to reduce them:
   a. Reduce the size of the chart to allow room for the bullet chart.
   b. Choose **Bullet Chart** from the **Insert** menu and draw a chart box the width of the slide.

   c. Compose the explanations and insert the text.
   d. Reduce the size of the bulleted text to fit comfortably at the bottom of the slide. Change the bullet style and color if desired.

7. Make any other adjustments desired to display both charts adequately on the slide.
8. Save the slide show as **ANNREPT.** Print Slides 1–3 as a handout with three slides per page and no background. (*Hint:* In the Print dialog box, deselect the check box for **Full Range** in the Slide Range area. Set 1 as the Start number and 3 as the End number.)
9. Close the file and exit Presentations.

LESSON 7

Creating and Enhancing Pie Charts

OBJECTIVES

After completing this lesson, you will be able to:

1. Create a pie chart.
2. Explode a slice of the pie.
3. Create multiple pies on one chart.
4. Create proportional multiple pies.
5. Create linked pie charts.

Estimated Time: 1 hour

INTRODUCTION

Pie charts show pictorially the relation of the parts to the whole. When statistics add up to 100% of the whole, a pie chart often best depicts the data.

Presentations offers a number of options for enhancing your pie chart. You can emphasize parts of the pie by using bright colors fading to more subdued colors. You can shade parts of the pie to distinguish between sections. To emphasize an important part of the pie, you can separate one or more slices from the rest of the pie.

CREATING A PIE CHART

Key words to look for when choosing a pie chart to represent your data are *share, percentage of total, market share, proportion,* or *specified percent.* When you are planning your pie chart, try to use no more than six segments. If you have more than six groupings of data, choose the five largest and group the rest together as *Others.*

To create a pie chart:

- Double-click in a data box to access the Data Chart dialog box.

  or

- Choose **Data Chart** from the **Insert** menu or select the **Chart Object tool** from the tool palette, then click the screen or draw a box with the hand pointer. The Data Chart dialog box appears.
- Choose **Pie** from the Chart Type list and click the type of pie chart you want in the gallery of choices.

EXERCISE 7-1

Create a slide show that contains a slide with a pie chart.

1. Start Presentations. In the Document Selection dialog box, select **Create a New Slide Show** and click **OK.**
2. In the New Slide Show dialog box, choose a master from the Master Gallery and select the **Title** template.
3. In the Title template screen, key the title and subtitle of the slide show:
   Title: **ShurSweet Ice Cream**
   Subtitle: **Sales Analysis—Your name**
4. Add a second slide that uses the Background template.
5. Create a pie chart:
   a. Choose **Data Chart** from the **Insert** menu and click the screen to create a full-page chart. The Data Chart dialog box appears.
   b. Choose **Pie** from the Chart Type list, and select the first pie in the top row of choices. Click **OK.**
   c. The datasheet appears.
6. Leave the datasheet on the screen for the next exercise.

NOTE

Make sure 3-D is **not** selected in the Data Chart dialog box.

Entering Data

The datasheet for a pie chart differs from that for a bar chart, as shown in Figure 7–1. The pie chart datasheet lets you enter data and specify labels for more than one pie. You can also specify entries for more than one pie in the Legend column. You can choose to have labels only, a legend only, both legends and labels, or neither legends nor labels. Your pie chart will be easier to understand, however, if you use a legend or labels to indicate what the pie slices represent.

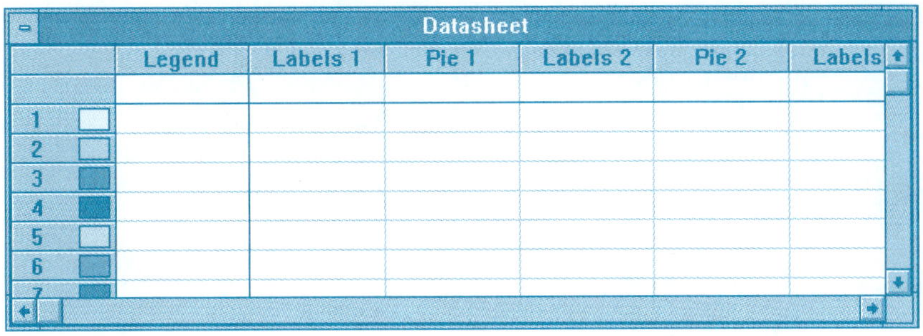

Figure 7–1
The datasheet for a pie chart

Most people usually follow a clockwise motion when viewing objects. Keep this in mind when deciding how to enter data into your pie chart. The first entry in the datasheet will appear at the 12 o'clock position, followed in counterclockwise order by the rest of your entries. If you want the largest segments of the pie to appear in clockwise order, you must enter them in *reverse* order following the first entry.

EXERCISE 7–2

Enter the data in the datasheet.

1. The data for the datasheet is listed below. Enter the flavors in the Legend column. Enter the numbers in the column headed *Pie 1.*

Chocolate	**3650**
Butter Pecan	**2250**
Strawberry	**2490**
Vanilla	**3220**

2. Your screen should resemble Figure 7–2 (on p. 96).
3. Close the chart editor. Save the new slide show as **SHRSALES** and leave it on the screen for the next exercise.

Displaying Labels

You can customize the way Presentations displays labels in a variety of ways. To change the way Presentations displays a label:

- Access the chart editor by double-clicking anywhere on the pie.
- In the chart editor, choose **Labels** from the **Chart** menu. The Pie Chart Labels dialog box shown in Figure 7–3 (on p. 96) appears.
- Select the desired options from the dialog box and click **OK.**

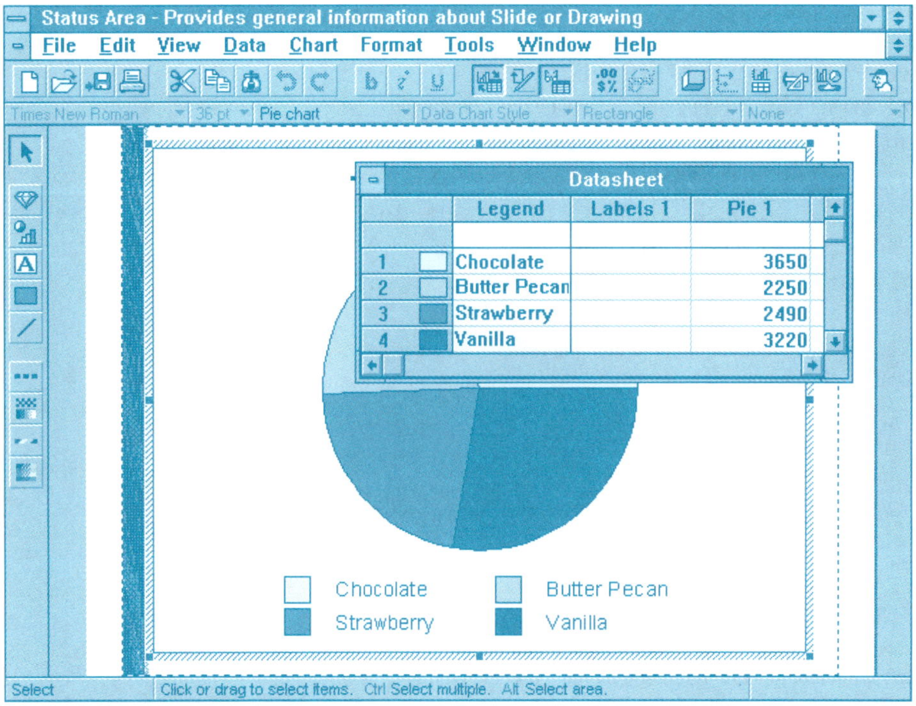

Figure 7–2
The completed datasheet

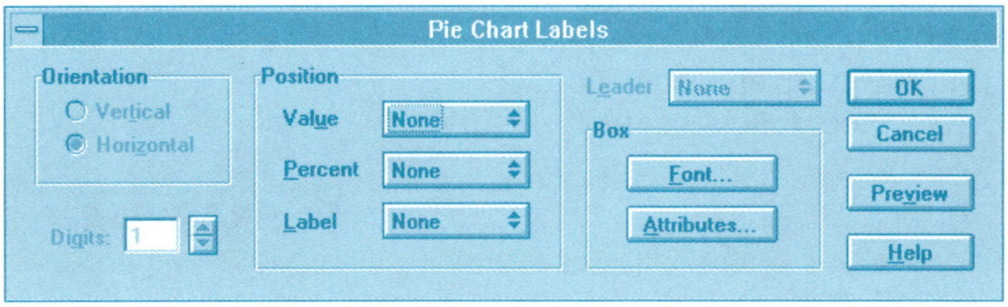

Figure 7–3
The Pie Chart Labels dialog box

The Pie Chart Labels dialog box provides a number of options for what kind of labels to display and how to display them. The Position area shows three command buttons, for Value, Percent, and Label. When you click on any of these buttons, hold down the mouse button to display a list box with Inside, Outside, and None as your choices. Selecting Inside or Outside for Value places the actual numbers you entered in the datasheet on the chart, either inside the pie slice that represents the value you entered, or outside the slice. Use the Percent button to display what percent of the whole each pie slice is. If you entered text in the Labels column of the datasheet, you can use the Label button to display the label. You can display each of these choices either vertically or horizontally.

Leader displays a short, medium, or long line extending from an outside label to the pie. The Box area provides options for changing the font and attributes of the label text.

EXERCISE 7–3

Change the display for the pie chart labels and add a title to the chart.

1. In the chart editor, choose **Labels** from the **Chart** menu. The Pie Chart Labels dialog box appears.
2. Click the **Percent** button and select **Outside.** Click **OK.**
3. Enter the title **Ice Cream Sales.**
4. Save the slide show and print it as a handout with no background.
5. Close the file and leave the Document Selection dialog box on the screen.

EDITING AND ENHANCING A PIE CHART

You can use skills you have already mastered in previous lessons to edit a pie chart:

- To *move* a pie chart, select it and drag it to a new location, as for any other object.
- To *resize* a pie chart, select it and drag handles to enlarge or shrink the chart. Dragging a corner handle will change both height and width.
- To *edit* any part of a pie chart, such as a slice or a label, double-click the object while in the chart editor.
- To change the pie chart from two-dimensional to three-dimensional, access the Data Chart dialog box or the Layout dialog box and click the **3-D** check box.

Presentations also allows you to make a number of enhancements to a basic pie chart. You can separate a pie slice from the whole pie to emphasize it. This is called *exploding* a slice. You can place more than one pie on a chart, and you can make the multiple pies proportional to one another. You can also link two pies in a number of ways.

Exploding a Pie Slice

Exploding a pie slice emphasizes the slice's importance. To explode a pie slice:

- In the chart editor, choose **Layout** from the **Chart** menu. The Pie Layout dialog box shown in Figure 7–4 (on p. 98) appears.
- In the Explode Slice section of the dialog box, specify the number of the slice you want to explode (the slices are numbered sequentially on the datasheet), then specify how far you want to separate it from the pie (measured in increments of 5).

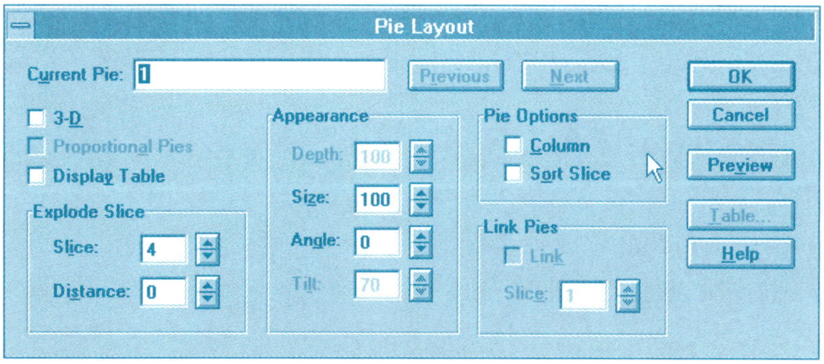

Figure 7–4
The Pie Layout dialog box

Use the exploded segment only to emphasize your message. Exploding too many pieces of the pie will make the chart difficult to read.

EXERCISE 7–4

In this exercise, you will work on a slide show that compares sales figures of ShurSweet's most popular ice creams over the course of a year. The data for January have been entered already in **EX7-4.SHW.** You will change the pie chart to 3-D and explode a slice.

1. In the Document Selection dialog box, choose **Work on an Existing File** and click **OK.**
2. In the Open File dialog box, retrieve **EX7-4.SHW** from your template disk.
3. Go to Slide 2. Select the chart and increase its size so it almost fills the screen.
4. Double-click on the pie to open the chart editor.
5. Choose **Layout** from the **Chart** menu.
6. Click the **3-D** check box at the top left of the Pie Layout dialog box.
7. In the Explode Slice section of the dialog box (bottom left corner), change Slice to **1** and Distance to **30**. Click **OK.**
8. Save the new slide show as **EDITPIE** and leave it on the screen for the next exercise.

Creating Multiple Pies on the Same Chart

You can display several pie charts on a single slide. The advantage to creating multiple pies is that you can compare wholes to wholes. For example, you can create a pie for each of two time periods so you can compare sales data from one period to the other.

When two charts are prepared from one datasheet, they act as one unit. This means you cannot move them or title them independently. If you need to position or title each pie, add a separate pie chart to a slide that already contains a pie chart.

Presentations lets you make some changes to each pie in a multiple pie chart. Clicking anywhere on one of the pies selects it, and the Pie Layout dialog box indicates the number of the current pie. This feature allows you to make changes such as exploding different pie slices from each pie and changing the size of one pie without changing the size of another.

To add data for multiple pies, simply retrieve the datasheet and update the data. Insert the new data in the Pie 2 column, and insert labels if necessary. If you want the new pie to share the same legend colors with the existing pie, use the same rows used by the existing pie. If you want to use new legend colors, begin your new data in rows below those already used.

EXERCISE 7-5

Add a second pie to the chart to represent the July sales data.

1. Open the chart editor for the chart in Slide 2.
2. Before adding the new pie, unexplode the slice in the current pie:
   a. Choose **Layout** from the **Chart** menu.
   b. Change Slice to **1** and Distance to **0.** Click **OK.**
3. Add data for the July sales figures:
   a. If the datasheet is not displayed, open it by choosing **Datasheet** from the **View** menu.
   b. The second pie uses the same legend as the first pie, so you just need to fill in the new sales figures.
   c. In the Pie 2 column, key the new sales figures:

Chocolate	**4230**
Butter Pecan	**2950**
Strawberry	**3050**
Vanilla	**3980**

4. Choose **Labels** from the **Chart** menu. Click the **Percent** button and choose the **Inside** option. Click **OK.**
5. Save the slide show and leave it on the screen for the next exercise.

Creating Proportional Pies

When you display several pies on one slide, you can make the pies *proportional.* Presentations sizes the pies according to the numbers entered in the datasheet. For example, when you compare the sales of ice cream in January and July, sales in July are greater. The month with the larger sales will result in a larger pie.

EXERCISE 7-6

Make the pies proportional.

1. Open the chart editor for the pies.
2. Choose **Layout** from the **Chart** menu.

3. Click the **Proportional Pies** check box, then click **OK.** Notice Pie 2 is larger than Pie 1.
4. Save the slide show and leave it open for the next exercise.

Changing Text Font and Attributes

You can change the font and attributes of any text or box on the chart, including titles, labels, and legends. To change text attributes:

- In the chart editor, double-click on the text you want to edit.
- For a title, click the **Options** button in the Title dialog box, then click the **Font** or **Attributes** button in the Title Options dialog box.
- For labels, click the **Font** or **Attributes** button in the Pie Chart Labels dialog box.
- For a legend, click the **Font** or **Attributes** button in the Legend dialog box.

Choosing any Font button displays the Font dialog box you have worked with before, where you can change the font, style, and size. Choosing any Attributes button displays a dialog box where you can select the box style that encloses the text, fill color that provides the background in the box, and border style and color. A Preview button allows you to see your changes as you make them.

EXERCISE 7-7

Change the text attributes of the pie labels and add a subtitle.

1. With the chart editor active, double-click any of the percent labels. The Pie Chart Labels dialog box appears.
2. Click the **Attributes** button to open the Box Attributes dialog box shown in Figure 7–5.

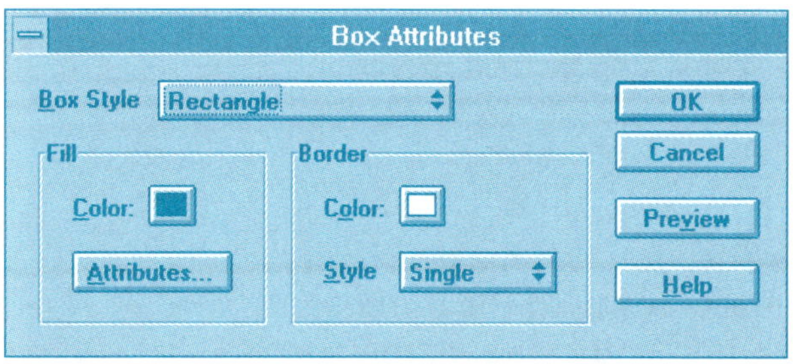

Figure 7–5
The Box Attributes dialog box

3. This dialog box currently indicates that labels are shown in a rectangular box, with a black fill and white border. Change the box attributes to no border and white fill:
   a. In the Fill area, click the box next to Color. Choose the white square at the top of the palette.
   b. In the Border area, click the **Style** button and choose **None.**
   c. Click **OK** to return to the Pie Chart Labels dialog box.

4. Change the color and size of the labels:
   a. Click the **Font** button.
   b. Select **20** from the Font Size list.
   c. Click the **Attributes** button at the right of the dialog box.
   d. Choose black for the foreground color and click the **Outline Off** check box.
   e. Click **OK** *three times.*
5. Add the subtitle **January and July Figures** and click **OK.**
6. Save the slide show and print it as a handout with two slides per page and no background.
7. Close the file and leave the Document Selection dialog box on the screen.

Linking Pies

You can link *a slice of the pie* to a breakdown of the contents of the slice. For example, you might want to link chocolate ice cream with the different varieties of chocolate ice cream to see which of the chocolate flavors is the best seller. Your message for that slide might be that Dutch chocolate has such a small share of the market, it does not pay to produce it. You are comparing *one slice* of the first pie to the *entire second pie.*

To link two pies:

- Insert data for the first pie.
- Add data for the second pie to the datasheet. For the second pie, you need to insert labels in the Labels 2 column, because the data entries will not be the same items as for the first pie.
- In the first pie, select the slice you want to link to the second pie.
- Choose **Layout** from the **Chart** menu and click in the **Link** check box.

When you link two pies in this fashion, the new pie linked to the slice of the first pie might be much larger than the first pie. You can change the size of the new pie by selecting **Proportional Pies** in the Pie Layout box or by decreasing the number in the Size box in the Appearance area of this dialog box.

EXERCISE 7-8

Link two pies.

1. Open **EX7-8.SHW** from your template disk.
2. Access the chart editor for the pie chart on Slide 2.
3. Choose **Datasheet** from the **View** menu and add the following data for Pie 2. Insert the flavors in the Labels 2 column, and the numbers in the Pie 2 column. Begin your entries in *Row 5* so the new pie slices will have different colors from those in Pie 1. When you finish adding the data, close the datasheet.

Mint Choc Chip	**1350**
Double Choc Chip	**1775**
Dutch Chocolate	**525**

4. Link the Chocolate slice in Pie 1 to the breakdown in Pie 2.
   a. Click the Chocolate slice in Pie 1 to select it.
   b. Choose **Layout** from the **Chart** menu. The Pie Layout dialog box appears.
   c. Click the **Link** check box, then click **OK.**
5. Your chart should resemble Figure 7–6.

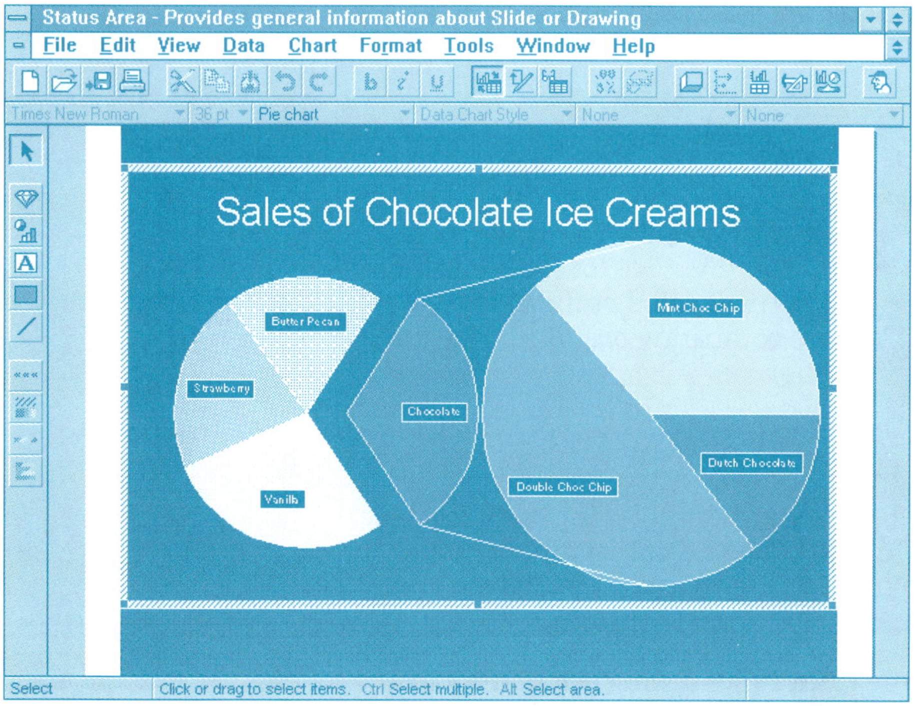

Figure 7–6
The linked pies

6. Enhance the appearance of the linked pies:
   a. Click anywhere on Pie 2 to select it.
   b. Choose **Layout** from the **Chart** menu again and click the **3-D** check box to make the pies three-dimensional.
   c. In the Appearance area, change the number in the Size box to **60.** Click **OK.**
   d. Select options from the Font and Attributes dialog boxes to make the labels more readable and attractive.
   e. In Pie 2, click each slice and change it to an appropriate color.
   f. When finished, click **OK** to return to the chart editor.
7. Save the slide show as **LINKPIE** and print it as a handout with two slides per page and no background.
8. Close the file and exit Presentations.

ACTIVITIES

TRUE/FALSE

In the blank space before each sentence, place a **T** if the statement is true and an **F** if it is false.

_____ 1. Pie charts represent the relation of parts to a whole.

_____ 2. Pie chart labels can be oriented vertically or horizontally.

_____ 3. If you want to use more than one pie on a slide, you can create multiple pies in the same chart, or you can create several independent pies on the same slide.

_____ 4. Presentations lets you "explode" a slice of a pie to emphasize the data the slice represents.

_____ 5. You cannot specify labels for more than one pie.

COMPLETION

Fill in the blank.

1. If you have multiple pies in the same chart and the size of the pies varies with the amount of data in each, the pies are _______________ .
2. The _______________ button places the numbers entered in the datasheet on the chart.
3. You can _______________ a slice of a pie to another pie that represents the breakdown of the contents of the slice.
4. The _______________ button lets you select box style and fill and the border color.
5. You can place labels, values, and _______________ inside or outside of the pie.

R E V I E W

REVIEW EXERCISE 7-1

The ShurSweet Ice Cream Company has introduced two new flavors, *Lime Cordial* and *Peanut Crunch*. The company has been testing the flavors along with three other recently introduced premium flavors in three cities for the past six months. The ShurSweet management wants to include in its annual report data on sales of the new flavors as a percentage of sales of all flavors in the test cities. Based on this chart, they will decide whether to manufacture the new flavors next year. Update the annual report slide show to show the data on a pie chart.

1. Start Presentations and retrieve **ANNREPT.SHW** from your data disk.
2. Use the Background template to add a new slide following the New Products title slide. Use the Slide Sorter view if necessary to make sure the new slide is positioned correctly.
3. On the new slide, create three pie charts to show the data below. Use one datasheet for all three pies. Do not insert labels, and place all flavor names in the Legend column. Place all data in Rows 1–5 so they will have the same legend colors.

	Duluth	**Memphis**	**Portland**
Lime Cordial	**220**	**370**	**150**
Peanut Crunch	**350**	**530**	**430**
Butter Brickle	**400**	**600**	**620**
Cherry Cheesecake	**350**	**525**	**750**
Chocolate Chunk	**450**	**720**	**490**

4. Add the title **Sales of New Flavors.**
5. Explode the pie slices representing the new flavors by clicking each pie and choosing **Layout** from the **Chart** menu. Explode slices 1 and 2 for each pie.
6. Show percents inside the slices. Edit the labels as desired to make them more attractive and readable.
7. Reduce the size of the title and the legend text to maximize the size of the pies. (*Hint:* To change the legend text font size, double-click any legend text and choose the **Series Font** box.)
8. Change the colors of the pie slices to match their flavors.

9. Make the pies three-dimensional.
10. Save the slide show as **ANNREPT2.** Print only the New Products title slide and the slide showing the pie charts.
11. Close the file and exit Presentations.

LESSON 8

Creating and Enhancing XY Charts

OBJECTIVES

After completing this lesson, you will be able to:

1. Create a line chart.
2. Change line style.
3. Add axis labels.
4. Change frame options.
5. Format tick marks and grid lines.

Estimated Time: 1 hour

INTRODUCTION

XY graphs show relationships between two variables. The *dependent variable* (a quantity that can change based on another value) is plotted on the *X-axis*. The X-axis is a *horizontal* line divided into segments. The *independent variable* is plotted on the *Y-axis* (a *vertical* line, also divided into segments based on the variable to be plotted on it).

The most commonly used XY charts are bar charts and line charts. You created bar charts in Lesson 6. In this lesson, you will create and enhance a line chart.

CREATING A LINE CHART

Line charts are particularly useful for showing *trends*—that is, how something changes over time. When statistics tend to steadily increase or decrease, line charts can graphically illustrate the trend. Line charts are also good for showing exceptions to trends. For example, stock prices might steadily increase until a new law proposed by Congress causes a panic among buyers for a month or two. Everyone wants to sell, causing prices to fall dramatically. When the effect of the new program is not as great as feared, the market stabilizes again. A line chart can clearly show the "spike" caused by the panic.

To create a line chart:

- Choose **Data Chart** from the **Insert** menu.

  or

- Select the **Chart Object tool** icon from the tool palette and click a slide to create a full-page chart or draw a box the size you want the chart to be.
- Choose **Line** in the Data Chart dialog box and select a type of line chart from the gallery of examples.

EXERCISE 8-1

Create a slide show that contains a slide with a line chart.

1. Start Presentations and begin a new slide show. Choose a master from the Master Gallery and begin the slide show with a Title slide.
2. Enter the title **ShurSweet Ice Cream** and the subtitle **Product Analysis—Your name.**
3. Add a second slide (use the Background template). Select the **Chart Object tool** from the tool palette and click the new slide to open the Data Chart dialog box.
4. Choose **Line** and select the first chart in the top row of chart types. Click **OK.** The datasheet appears.
5. Leave the datasheet on the screen for the next exercise.

NOTE

Make sure 3-D is **not** selected in the Data Chart dialog box.

Entering the Data

The datasheet for a line chart (Figure 8–1) is similar to the datasheet for a bar chart. Note that you can enter labels and legends for only one set of data. Also, the line chart datasheet does not specify colors for legend entries. Rather, the lines appear with differing patterns. You can, however, change line colors when you edit the line chart.

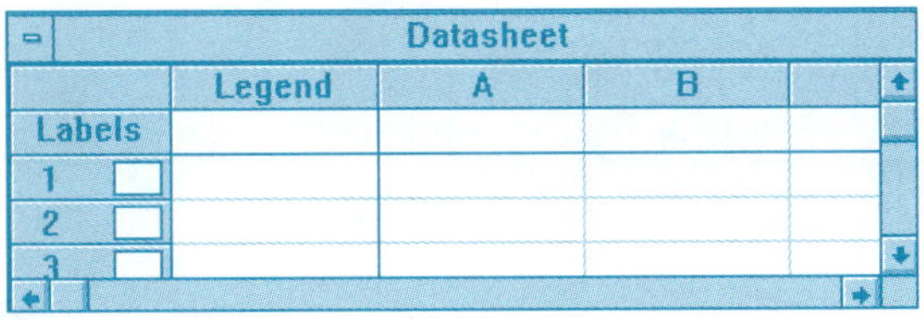

Figure 8–1
The line chart datasheet

EXERCISE 8–2

Enter the data for the line chart.

1. In the datasheet, enter the following data. Enter the flavors in the Legend column and begin the month labels in Column A.

	Jan.	Mar.	May	Jul.	Sep.	Nov.
Orange	560	575	750	650	730	700
Lemon	500	490	600	700	690	660
Rainbow	400	425	550	600	550	525
Strawberry	200	250	500	600	600	600

2. The line chart appears on the screen as you enter the data. Close the datasheet.
3. Add the title **Sherbet Sales.**
4. Save the slide show as **SHERSALE** and leave it on the screen for the next exercise.

Changing Line Styles and Colors

By default, Presentations chooses line patterns and a single color—white—to represent your data. You can change a line's pattern, thickness, and color to customize your line chart.

To change line styles and color:

- In the chart editor, double-click the line you want to change in the chart. The Series Options dialog box shown in Figure 8–2 appears.

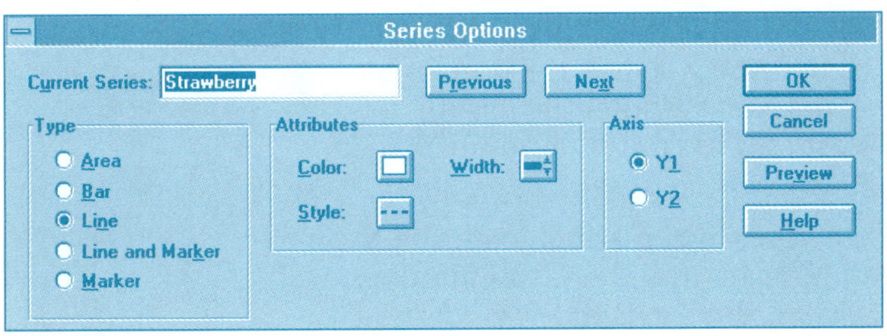

Figure 8–2
The Series Options dialog box

- In the Attributes area, click the **Color** button to display a color palette to choose from. Click the **Width** button to select a line weight. Click the **Style** button to select a line style.

EXERCISE 8-3

Change the line styles, width, and color.

1. Double-click the chart to open the chart editor.
2. Double-click any line in the chart. The Series Options dialog box appears.
3. The flavor name appears in the text box at the top of the dialog box. Choose a color to match the flavor. (You'll need to use your imagination for Rainbow!)
4. Click the **Width** button and pick the fifth option in the top row to produce a heavier line.
5. Click the **Style** button and select the first choice, the solid line.
6. Click **OK** and note that the line and the legend have changed.
7. Repeat Steps 2–6 for the other lines on the chart.
8. Save the slide show. Print the slide show as a handout with two slides per page and no background.
9. Leave the slide show on the screen for the next exercise.

NOTE

You can use the Previous and Next buttons next to the text box containing the flavor name to choose another "flavor" without closing the dialog box each time.

EDITING AND ENHANCING AN XY CHART

Use the skills you have already learned to edit a line chart. Moving and resizing are the same for a line chart as for a pie chart. You also change font and attributes for titles and labels in the same way as for any other kind of chart: In the chart editor, double-click the element you want to edit and make choices from the dialog boxes that appear. To change the chart type or dimension, open the Data Chart dialog box and select the new chart type and/or the 3-D check box.

Presentations also offers some special editing and enhancing features for XY charts. Although you will use a line chart to explore these options, they are also available for bar charts and other types of XY charts.

Adding Axis Titles

Earlier in this lesson, you learned that the X-axis is the horizontal axis. In the chart on your screen, the X-axis shows the month labels. The Y-axis, or vertical axis, shows the range of numbers that the data entries fall within.

You can add *axis titles* to give further information about the X- and Y-axes. For example, you can indicate that the Y-axis numbers represent thousands of units. Labeling the Y-axis this way lets you use smaller numbers to create the chart.

To add an axis title:

- In the chart editor, double-click the title or choose **Titles** from the **Chart** menu. The Titles dialog box shown in Figure 8–3 appears. This dialog box lets you insert a title in both the Y1 Axis and X Axis boxes, as well as in the Title and Subtitle boxes.
- Choose the **Options** button with a title selected for further options for the appearance of the title.

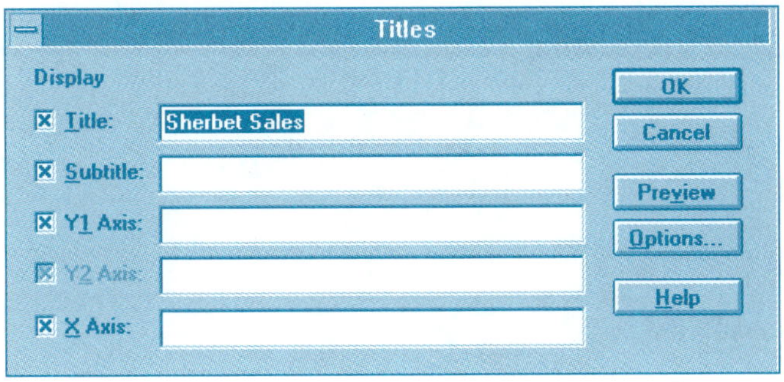

Figure 8–3
The Titles dialog box for XY charts

EXERCISE 8–4

Add axis titles to the line chart on your screen.

1. In the chart editor, double-click the title to open the Titles dialog box.
2. In the Y1 Axis box, key **In 1000s.**
3. In the X Axis box, key the current year.
4. Click the **Preview** button and view your axis titles. They look fine, but don't stand out from the other labels.
5. Click the **Options** button to display the Titles Options dialog box. Select the **Y1 Axis** option button if it is not already selected and then choose the **Font** button to display the Font dialog box.
6. Select **Bold** Font Style and click **OK.**
7. Repeat this process for the X Axis title. Click **OK** until you return to the chart editor.
8. Save the slide show and leave it on the screen for the next exercise.

Changing the Frame

The *frame* of an XY chart consists of the Y-axis line, the X-axis line, the top line, and the right line (if the chart type has a right line) that enclose the chart. The frame also includes a fill color or pattern that appears behind the chart elements. The chart currently on your screen has a black fill and white frame lines at the top, left, and bottom. You can change the color of these frame elements, or you can eliminate them to give your chart a more customized look.

To change a frame element:

- In the chart editor, double-click any area of the frame fill (the black area). The Frame dialog box appears as shown in Figure 8–4 (on p. 112).

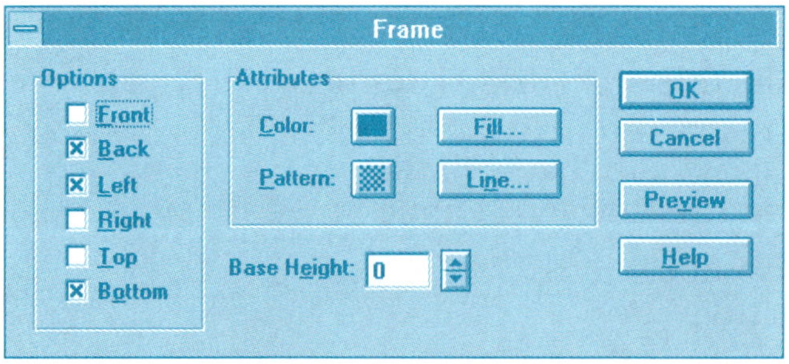

Figure 8–4
The Frame dialog box

- In the Options area, click check boxes to display or remove frame lines as desired.
- In the Attributes area, click the **Fill** button to change the color and pattern of the fill. Click **Line** to change the line style, weight, and color.

Changing the Grid and Tick Marks

The *grid* is the series of horizontal and vertical lines that mark increments on the X- and Y-axes. Some Presentations charts have only horizontal grid lines, while others have both horizontal and vertical grid lines. *Tick marks* are the small lines that extend from the axis labels to the axes themselves. Presentations lets you change color, style, and location for both grid lines and tick marks.

To change the grid and tick marks:

- In the chart editor, double-click a grid line or a tick mark. The Grid and Tick Options dialog box appears, as shown in Figure 8–5.
- Click the option button for the axis you want to change.
- In the Major area, click the **Grid** button to change grid lines. Click the **Tick** button to change the position of the tick marks. Click the **Color** button to change the color of both grid lines and tick marks.

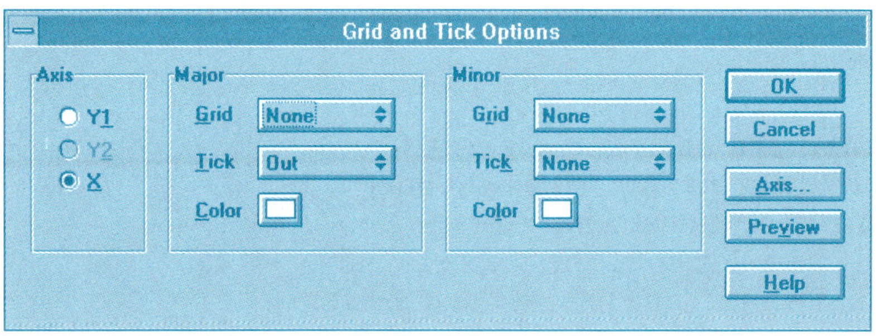

Figure 8–5
The Grid and Tick Options dialog box

EXERCISE 8–5

Change the frame fill and the grid line style.

1. In the chart editor, double-click anywhere in the black fill area of the chart. The Frame dialog box appears.
2. Click the **Fill** button. In the Fill Attributes dialog box, select the **None** option button in the Fill Type area to remove the fill entirely.

3. Click **OK** *twice* to return to the chart editor.
4. Double-click any grid line or tick mark. The Grid and Tick Options dialog box appears.
5. Click the **Grid** button and select **Dashed.** Click **OK** to return to the chart editor.
6. Save the slide show and leave it on the screen for the next exercise.

Editing the Legend

Legends are available with all types of charts; you have worked briefly with them in previous lessons. You can customize a chart's legend in much the same way you edit titles and labels.

To edit a legend:

- In the chart editor, double-click anywhere on the legend. The Legend dialog box appears as shown in Figure 8–6.
- In the Legend dialog box, you can choose a position for the legend. You can also change the font and select box attributes for it. If you wish, you can give the legend a title that displays above it.

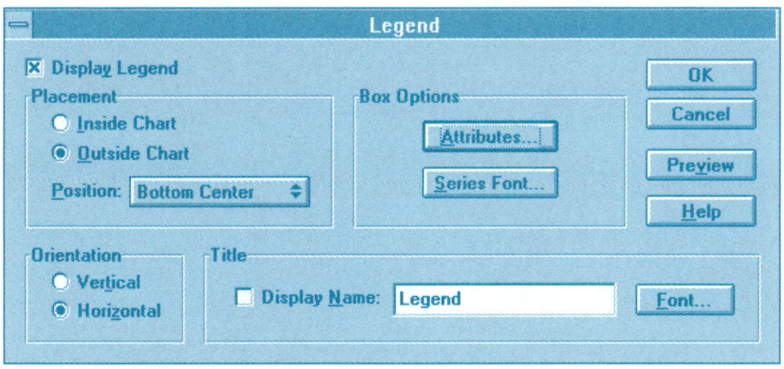

Figure 8–6
The Legend dialog box

EXERCISE 8–6

Change the position of the legend and give it a title.

1. In the chart editor, double-click the legend to display the Legend dialog box.
2. Click the **Position** button and select **Bottom Left** from the list box.
3. In the Title text box (it currently displays *Legend*), key **Sherbet Flavors**. Click the **Display Name** check box to the left of the text box. Click **OK**.
4. Save the slide show. Print the slide show as a handout with two slides per page and no background.
5. Close the file and exit Presentations.

ACTIVITIES

MULTIPLE CHOICE

Choose the *best answer* to each of the following questions.

_____ 1. XY graphs show the relationship:
   a. of the parts to the whole
   b. between two variables
   c. both
   d. neither

_____ 2. You change the line pattern for a line chart in the:
   a. Frame dialog box
   b. Titles text box
   c. Series Options dialog box
   d. Chart Type list box

_____ 3. The X-axis represents the range of values for the:
   a. independent variable
   b. dependent variable
   c. intervening variable
   d. none of the above

_____ 4. Which type of chart or graph is particularly good for showing *trends*?
   a. Line graph
   b. Bar chart
   c. Pie chart
   d. Scatter chart

_____ 5. A tick mark is a:
   a. horizontal or vertical line that marks increments on an axis
   b. small line that extends from an axis label to the axis
   c. square that indicates a chart is selected
   d. pointer you use to draw a chart box

COMPLETION

Fill in the blank.

1. A/an ________________ shows how something changes over time.
2. The X-axis is a/an ________________ line divided into segments.
3. A/an ________________ gives further information about the X- or Y-axis.
4. The ________________ of an XY chart consists of the axis lines and a fill color.
5. The ________________ is a series of horizontal and/or vertical lines that mark increments on the X- and Y-axes.

REVIEW

REVIEW EXERCISE 8-1

For the ShurSweet annual report, ShurSweet management wants to include a chart showing trends in product sales over the previous year. Update the annual report slide show to show the data on a line chart.

1. Start Presentations and retrieve **ANNREPT2.SHW** from your data disk.
2. Use the Background template to add a new slide following the Sales Trends title slide. Use the Slide Sorter view if necessary to be sure the new slide is positioned correctly.
3. Create a line chart on the new slide and insert the following data:

	Quarter 1	Quarter 2	Quarter 3	Quarter 4
Ice Cream	**176**	**190**	**250**	**230**
Sherbet	**110**	**140**	**210**	**180**
Frozen Yogurt	**95**	**110**	**150**	**130**

4. Add the following titles and use the bold style:

   Title: **Product Sales**

   Y1 Axis: **1000s of Units**

   X Axis: **Current Year**

5. Make the chart three-dimensional and remove the frame fill.
6. Reduce the size of the X-axis and Y-axis labels. (*Hint:* Click any number or *Quarter* label.) Reduce the size of the legend font so the legend fits on one line. (*Hint:* Click the Series Font button in the Legend dialog box to access a Font dialog box.)
7. Select colors of your choice for the lines.
8. Save the slide show as **ANNREPT3.** Print only the Sales Trends title slide and the slide showing the line chart.
9. Close the file and exit Presentations.

LESSON 9

Creating and Enhancing Organization Charts

OBJECTIVES

After completing this lesson, you will be able to:

1. Create an organization chart.
2. Understand organizational structure.
3. Add entries and change the top position on the organization chart.
4. Change the orientation of an organization chart.

Estimated Time: 1 hour

INTRODUCTION

An organization chart (Figure 9–1) shows the chain of command in an organization. The basic chart shows how people or activities relate to one another in the structure of an organization. The typical organization chart depicts the relationship of individuals in an organization and to whom they report in a company or a department. You might also use an organization chart to show the relationship of departments in an organization or the individuals in one department.

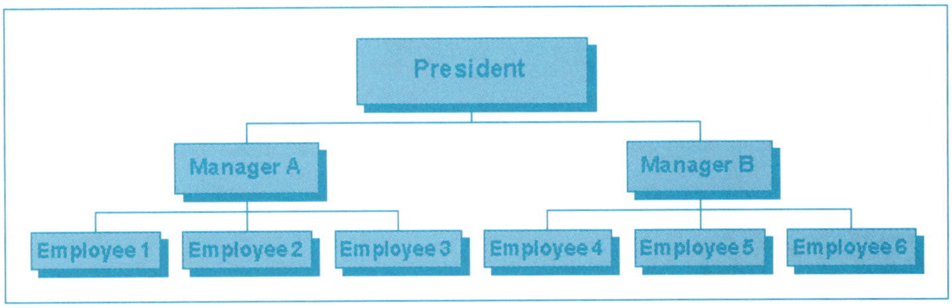

Figure 9–1
Organization chart

Typically, an organization chart begins with a single box at the top of a pyramid representing the president or CEO. Smaller boxes below show who is subordinate to whom.

You can also use the organization chart format for other applications. For example, you can use this type of chart to show the structure of a unit or a department, to depict a flow of activity in a work system, or to design a family tree.

CREATING AN ORGANIZATION CHART

A chart that starts at the top and works down is usually easiest to follow. Though most organization charts are laid out top to bottom, Presentations also lets you display your chart bottom to top, left to right, or right to left.

You create organization charts in the Outline box displayed after you access the chart editor. The Outline box is similar to the Outliner, only smaller. However, data you enter in the Outline box does not appear in the Outliner when you switch views.

You can add other charts or tables to your organization chart, but you cannot create two organization charts on one slide.

To create an organization chart:

- Select the **Org Chart** template to open a working screen with boxes for title, subtitle, and the organization chart.

  or

- Choose **Organization Chart** from the **Insert** menu, or select the **Organization Chart tool** from the tool palette. (Hold down the mouse button on the **Chart Object tool** icon to see the Organization Chart tool.)

- Click the preformatted organization chart box, click the slide with the **Organization Chart tool**, or draw a chart box with the hand pointer to open the Organization Chart dialog box shown in Figure 9–2.

Organization Chart

- Choose a chart style and click **OK** to display the Outline box.

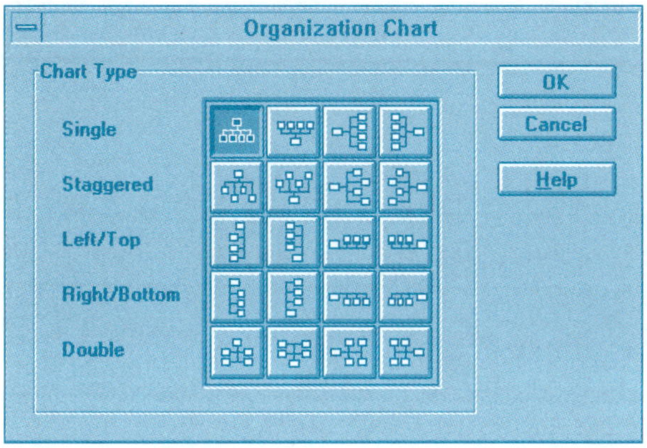

Figure 9–2
The Organization Chart dialog box

EXERCISE 9–1

Begin a new slide show that will contain an organization chart of the ShurSweet Company's accounting department.

1. Start Presentations and select **Create a New Slide Show** in the Document Selection dialog box. Click **OK** in the New Slide Show dialog box.
2. On the Title slide, enter **ShurSweet Ice Cream Company** as the title. Enter **Accounting Structure** as the subtitle.
3. Add one slide with the Background template.
4. Select the **Chart Objects tool** icon and hold the mouse button down to select the **Organization Chart tool.** Click the new slide. The Organization Chart dialog box appears.
5. The default organization chart style is selected. Click **OK** to accept this style.
6. The Outline box for the organization chart appears. Leave it on the screen for the next exercise.

Understanding Organizational Structure

Figure 9–3 (on p. 122) shows the Outline box as it appears after you select an organization chart type. Note that Presentations includes sample data to show you how an organization chart is structured.

Presentations uses the first entry in the Outline as the top of the chart. This entry usually represents the most important position or item in the organization chart. The Outline indicates this with the word *Top* at the left of the double rule.

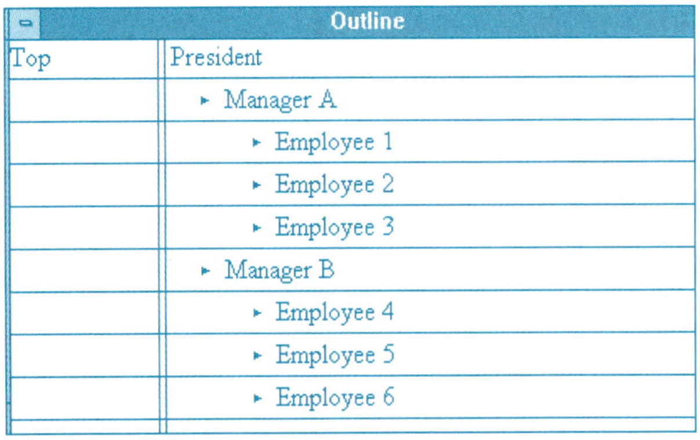

Figure 9–3
The Outline box

Entries below the top position are *subordinate* to it. In Figure 9–3, for example, the Manager A and Manager B positions are subordinate to the President position. In turn, subordinate entries can be *superior* to other entries. The position of Manager A, for example, is superior to those of Employees 1, 2, and 3.

Not shown in the sample data is an example of a *staff* position. A staff person is considered to be a support person for someone in the organization chart. Staff persons include assistants and secretaries. Presentations has a special method of showing how a staff person fits into the structure, which you will learn later in this lesson.

Entering the Data

Before you enter data into the Outline box, you should first delete the sample data. Otherwise, that data might become part of your organization chart.

To delete the sample data:

- Choose **Clear All** from the **Edit** menu.
- When the warning box asks if you want to clear the contents of the outline, choose **Yes.**

Entering data in the Outline box is similar to entering data in the Outliner. After you have entered the data for the top position, pressing Enter moves the cursor to the next line and automatically indents it for a subordinate position. After you have entered data for the first subordinate position, pressing Enter moves the cursor to the next line and maintains the same indent for another position at the same level. To indicate a further level of subordination, press Tab to move the indent to the right. To move to a superior level, press Shift+Tab to move the cursor back to the left.

The Outline box also lets you enter additional lines of text for an entry without automatically indenting them as new subordinate entries. To add text for an entry, press Enter to move to the next line, then press Backspace. The cursor stays on the same indent level as the entry for which you want to add text.

EXERCISE 9-2

Add data for the organization chart.

1. Delete the sample data:
   a. Choose **Clear All** from the **Edit** menu.
   b. Click **Yes** to clear the sample data from the outline.
2. With the cursor on the first line of the Outline, enter information about the head of accounting:
   a. Key the name of the head of accounting: **Amy Jo Wright.**
   b. Press **Enter** to move to the next line, then press **Backspace** to enter further text for this position.
   c. Key the position name: **Comptroller.**
   d. Press **Enter** and then **Backspace** to add further text.
   e. Key Ms. Wright's room number: **Room 246.**
   f. Press **Enter** to move to the next level of subordination.
3. As you complete each line, Presentations inserts the data into the chart behind the Outline box. Your screen should look like Figure 9–4.

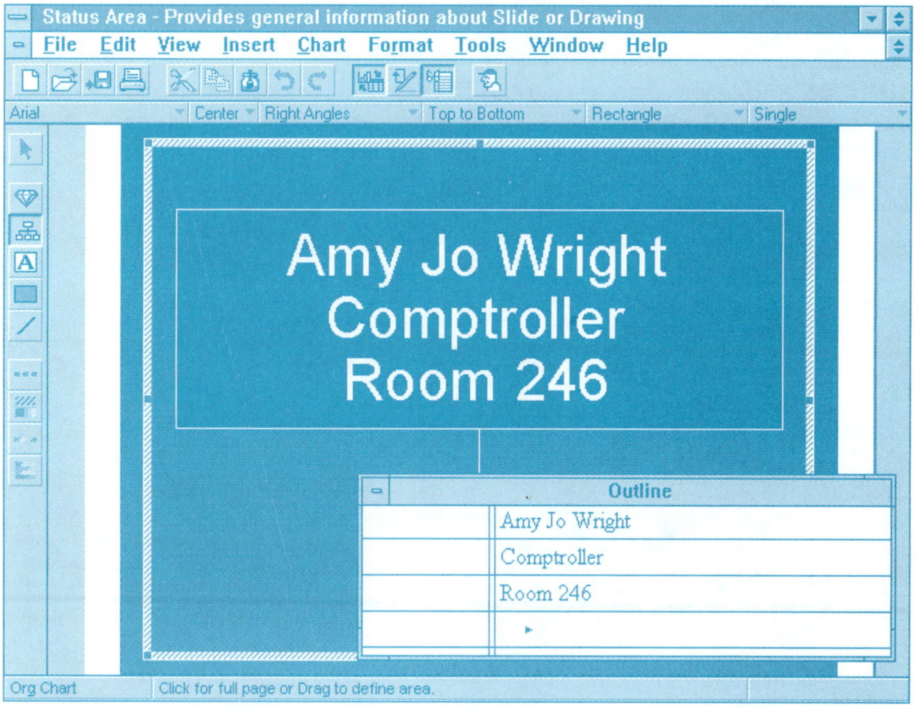

Figure 9–4
The top position entry

4. Following Steps 2a–2f, enter the data for an employee at the first level of subordination under the top position: **Brad Collins**, **Chief Financial Officer**, **Room 345.**
5. When you complete this entry, press **Enter** to move to the next line and then press **Tab** to move to the next level of subordination.
6. Enter the data for an employee subordinate to Mr. Collins: **Alma Smith**, **Assistant Financial Officer**, **Room 312.**
7. Press **Enter** and enter the data for an employee at the same level of subordination as Ms. Smith: **Marybeth Allen, Account Executive**, **Room 415.**

8. Press **Enter** and **Tab** to enter the data for an employee subordinate to Ms. Allen: **William Hilton**, **Assistant Account Executive, Room 420.**
9. You have completed listing the employees subordinate to Mr. Collins. You now need to indicate another branch of the organizational chart that is subordinate to Ms. Wright's position.
10. Press **Enter,** then press **Shift+Tab** *twice* to return to the first level of subordination. Enter data for this position: **Callan Sterling, Treasurer**, **Room 255.**
11. Press **Enter** and then **Tab** to move to the next level of subordination and enter data for an employee subordinate to Ms. Sterling: **Ralph Edwards, Assistant Treasurer**, **Room 263.**
12. Check your entries in the Outline box to make sure you have the correct subordination, then close the chart editor by clicking elsewhere on the screen.
13. Your organization chart appears in the chart editor as shown in Figure 9–5.
14. Save the slide show as **SHURORG** and leave it on the screen for the next exercise.

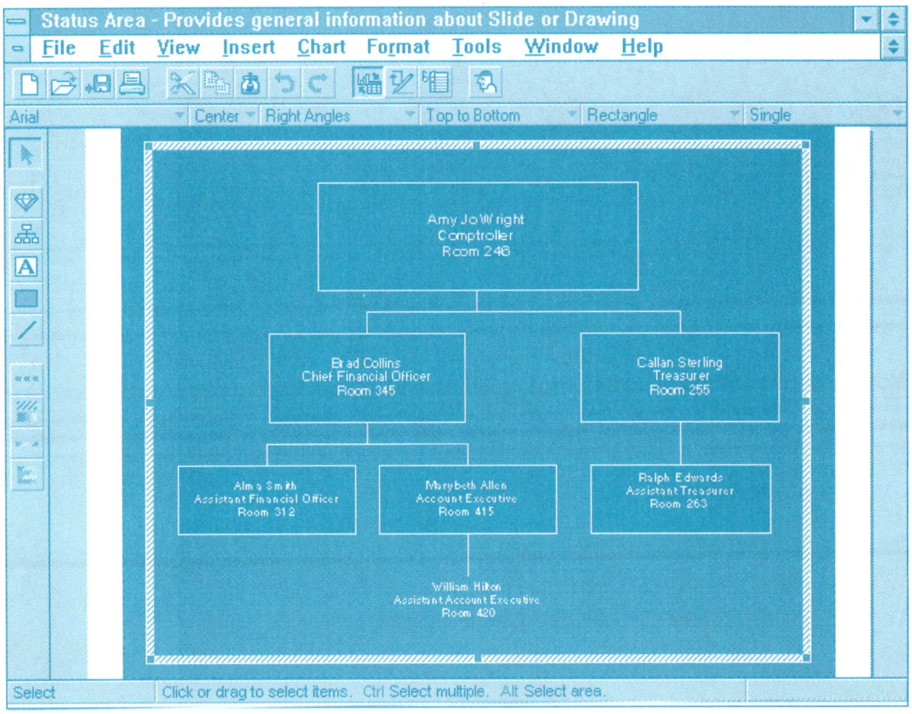

Figure 9–5
The completed organization chart

EDITING AND ENHANCING AN ORGANIZATION CHART

As with other chart types, you edit an organization chart while in the chart editor. By redisplaying the Outline box, you can easily make changes to the organization chart. You can add or delete entries, or change the level of subordination of any entry in the Outline box. You can also add staff positions and change the top position.

While creating or working with the organization chart, you can switch to a different layout choice at any time to change the way your chart displays on the slide.

Presentations offers many of the same enhancement features for organization charts that it offers for other charts. You can change the color of the fill for the boxes, for example, as well as the color of the lines that connect the boxes, called *connectors*. You can also change line thickness, box style, and font.

Adding, Deleting, and Changing Subordination of Entries

To add an entry:

- In the chart editor, choose **Outline** from the **View** menu.
- Place the cursor at the end of the entry *above* where you want the new entry. Press **Enter** to create the new entry.

To delete an entry:

- In the Outline box, drag to highlight the text of the entry you want to delete.
- Press **Backspace** *three* times to clear the text, remove the box, and remove the indent.

To change subordination of an entry:

- In the Outline box, place the cursor at the beginning of the line you want to change.
- Press **Tab** to move the entry to the right, making it more subordinate.
- Press **Shift+Tab** to move the entry to the left, making it more superior.

Adding a Staff Position

Staff positions are not considered part of the formal structure of an organization, so Presentations sets them off in a special way with a dashed or dotted line extending from the box of the staff person to the connector of the staff person's superior. You add a staff position *below* the last subordinate for the staff person's superior.

To add a staff entry to an organization chart:

- Position the cursor *after* the last subordinate of the staff person's superior and press **Enter.**

- Choose **Staff** from the **Chart** menu. The word *Staff* appears in the Outline box to the left of the double line.
- Enter the data for the staff person.

In the resulting organization chart, the staff person's box is connected by a dashed or dotted line to the connector of the superior.

Changing the Top Position

You can easily change the organization chart to show a different top position. To move a subordinate to the top position:

- Place the cursor in the entry you want to move to the top of the organization chart.
- Choose **Set Top** from the **Chart** menu. The word *Top* in the left margin of the Outline indicates the new top of the organization chart. All entries above the new top will not appear on the organization chart, and all subordinate entries below the new top move up one level of subordination.

EXERCISE 9-3

Add a staff position and practice changing the top position.

1. Click the **Select Object** icon on the tool palette and double-click on the organization chart to open the chart editor.
2. Add a staff position reporting to Callan Sterling:
   a. Position the cursor at the end of the last line of text for Ralph Edwards (following *Room 263*). Press **Enter.**
   b. Choose **Staff** from the **Chart** menu. The word *Staff* appears in the left margin of the Outline.
   c. Key the following data for the staff employee: **Eric O'Reilly, Administrative Secretary.**
3. Change the top position:
   a. Place the cursor in the line containing the name **Brad Collins.**
   b. Choose **Set Top** from the **Chart** menu.
   c. Note how the entries for Amy Jo Wright and Callan Sterling (and her subordinates) disappear from the chart on the screen and Mr. Collins's subordinates move up one level.
   d. Make Ms. Wright's position the top position again.
4. Save the slide show and leave it on the screen for the next exercise.

Changing the Appearance of the Organization Chart

To change the appearance of the organization chart, use the commands on the Chart and Format menus. These commands will be familiar to you from formatting other types of charts.

To change appearance:

- Choose **Box Attributes** from the **Chart** menu to change box style, outline style and color, and fill color.

- Choose **Box Options** from the **Chart** menu to control how boxes and the text within them display.
- Choose **Connectors** from the **Chart** menu to change the type and color of connector displays as well as the staff line style.
- Choose **Font** from the **Format** menu to select a font and a color for the font.

NOTE

You cannot change font size for an organization chart.

EXERCISE 9-4

Change the box appearance for the organization chart.

1. In the chart editor, choose **Box Attributes** from the **Chart** menu.
2. Choose a different color for the box fill. Make sure you can still read the text against the new color.
3. Change the border style to **Shadow** and change the border color if desired. Click **OK.**
4. Note that William Hilton's entry is not boxed. To box his entry, choose **Box Options** from the **Chart** menu. In the Display area, choose the **All Levels** option button. This displays a box for everyone on the organization chart. Click **OK.**
5. Save the slide show and leave it on the screen for the next exercise.

Changing the Orientation of the Organization Chart

If after creating an organization chart you decide you want to change the way it displays, you can select a new display using one of the following methods:

- Choose **Gallery** from the **Chart** menu and choose a new display from the listed styles.
- Choose **Layout** from the **Chart** menu and select a new orientation in the Layout dialog box.
- Click on the **Chart Orientation** button on the Power Bar for a list of available orientations.

Chart Orientation

EXERCISE 9-5

Change the orientation of the organization chart.

1. In the chart editor, choose **Gallery** from the **Chart** menu.
2. Select the third sample in the top row and click **OK.**
3. Save the slide show. Print it as a handout with two slides per page and no background.
4. Close the file and exit Presentations.

A C T I V I T I E S

TRUE/FALSE

In the blank space before each sentence, place a **T** if the statement is true and an **F** if it is false.

______ 1. Organization charts are always displayed top to bottom.

______ 2. The Outline box is exactly the same as the Outliner view.

______ 3. A staff employee is a support person for someone in an organization.

______ 4. You can use an organization chart to create a family tree.

______ 5. You cannot change the top position in the Outline box.

COMPLETION

Fill in the blank.

1. Organization charts are usually oriented ________________ .
2. The first entry in the Outline box is the ________________ .
3. A/an ________________ entry appears in the Outline below and indented to the right of the entry above it.
4. To make an entry superior, place the cursor at the beginning of the line and press________________ .
5. The ________________ dialog box controls how boxes and the text within them display.

REVIEW

REVIEW EXERCISE 9-1

The ShurSweet Company wants to include in their annual report an organization chart that depicts the branch locations of the company and their managers. Update the annual report slide show and create an organization chart for the management to review.

1. Start Presentations and retrieve **ANNREPT3.SHW** from your data disk.
2. Add a new slide following the Company Organization title slide. Use the Background template. You can use the Slide Sorter view to make sure you have added the new slide in the proper location.
3. Create an organization chart on the new slide and enter the data shown below for the company's locations. Levels of subordination are indicated by indents.

    Main Headquarters
    Fifth and Broadway
    - **Downtown Loop**
      1325 Madison Avenue
        - **Ann Jones**
          Manager
    - **Des Plaines**
      10345 Ryder Road
        - **Lena Johnson**
          Manager
    - **Highland Hills**
      2387 Western Row
        - **Robert Falls**
          Manager
    - **Gary**
      87 West Fourth Street
        - **James O. Webb**
          Manager

4. Enhance the organization chart by changing the box fill color and border style. Make sure all entries have boxes.
5. Change the connector color if desired.
6. Change the font, font style, and color if desired.
7. Save the slide show as **ANNRPT4A.** Print only the slide showing the organization chart.
8. Close the file.

REVIEW EXERCISE 9-2

The ShurSweet management has reviewed the organization chart and decided to add the Assistant Managers to the chart. Update the annual report to show the additional personnel on the organization chart.

1. Retrieve **ANNRPT4A.SHW** from your data disk.
2. Add the Assistant Managers listed below in their proper locations and levels of subordination. Don't forget to enter the title *Assistant Manager* for each.

Downtown Loop:	**Joseph Cranshaw**
	Marybeth Smith
Des Plaines:	**Allison North**
	Baxter Clark
Highland Hills:	**Ralph Durand**
	Alice Thames
Gary:	**Philip Matson**
	Burton Jackson

3. Save the slide show as **ANNREPT4.** Print only the Company Organization title slide and the slide containing the revised organization chart.
4. Close the file and exit Presentations.

LESSON 10

Adding Transitions and Making the Presentation

OBJECTIVES

After completing this lesson, you will be able to:

1. Choose transition options for your slide show.
2. Advance your slides automatically.
3. Add sound effects to your slides.
4. Make your presentation!

Estimated Time: 1 hour

INTRODUCTION

When you have finished preparing your slides, you can put the finishing touches on your work. Adding visual and/or sound effects to your slides can add emphasis, keep your audience focused on your current topic, or help you grab attention.

ADDING TRANSITIONS TO A SLIDE SHOW

The most important visual effect that Presentations offers is the *transition*. A transition is the way one slide changes to another. In the slide shows you have played up to now, the transition has been *Normal*—that is, one slide displays, disappears from view, and is replaced by another. Presentations provides ten more ways to specify how slides change. These transitions are described in Table 10–1. Some transition types give you further control options after you choose them.

Type	Function
Normal	Does not add any transition to the slide.
Wipe	Displays and removes ("wipes") the slide from **right, left, up,** or **down**.
Open	**Vertical** or **horizontal** "wipe" across the screen, like a window shade.
Close	The same as open, but the "window shade" closes.
Box	A large rectangle shrinks **in** or a small rectangle expands **out**.
Spots	The slide appears and disappears in **Fine**, **Small**, **Medium**, **Large**, or **Xlarge** dots.
Blinds	**Vertical** or **horizontal** bars similar to window blinds open or close the screen.
Jigsaw	The slide appears to break into **small**, **medium,** or **large** pieces of a jigsaw puzzle.
Snake	A "snake" moving **right**, **left**, **up**, or **down** wipes the slide off the screen.
Diagonal	A diagonal line moving **right-up, right-down, left-up,** or **left-down** wipes the slide off the screen.
Overwrite	The new slide overwrites the last slide.

Table 10–1
Presentations transition types

As a general rule, you should limit transitions in a slide show to one or two of these options. Using too many transition options can create a chaotic effect.

Presentations also offers three other visual effects. The *Overlay* effect lets you place one slide on top of another so both slides are displayed simultaneously. The *Cascade Bullets* effect displays bullets at your direction, so you can present the material in each bullet separately. If you also choose the Transition Bullets check box, any transition you have applied to the slide will also apply to the cascading bullets. That is, if your slide transition is Wipe, the bullets will be "wiped" onto the slide in the same way.

NOTE

Only bullets created using the Bullet Chart template will cascade.

To add transitions and other visual effects to your slides:

- Choose **Transition** from the **Slide** menu.

  or

- Select the **Transition** icon from the Toolbar. The Slide Transition dialog box shown in Figure 10–1 appears.

Transition

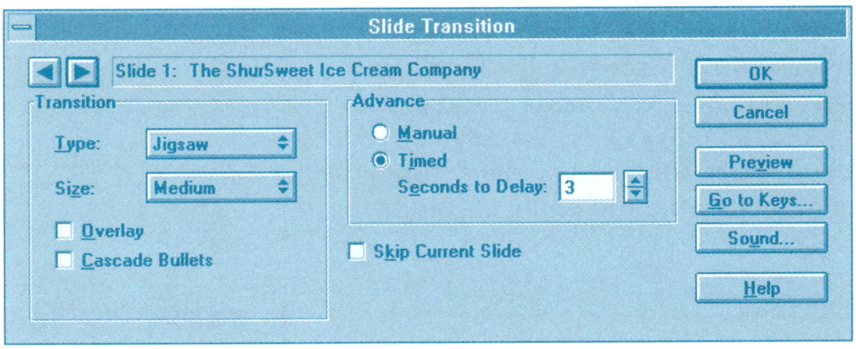

Figure 10–1
Slide Transition dialog box

- Choose the slide number using the left and right arrow buttons at the top of the dialog box.
- Click the **Type** button to select the type of transition you want to apply to the selected slide.
- Click the **Preview** button to see the transition you have chosen without having to play the entire slide show.

EXERCISE 10–1

Add transitions to an existing slide show.

1. Start Presentations and retrieve **EX10-1.SHW** from your template disk.
2. Review the slide show to determine what kind of visual effects might be appropriate.
3. Add a different transition to each slide for practice:
   a. Choose **Transition** from the **Slide** menu. The Slide Transition dialog box appears.
   b. Make sure the arrow button at the top of the dialog box indicates Slide 1.

c. Select a transition by clicking the **Type** button. If the transition you choose offers further choices, select one of the options.
d. Preview the transition by clicking the **Preview** button.
e. Select cascading bullets for the slides that have bullet charts.
f. When you are satisfied with the transition, choose transitions for the other slides.

4. Click **OK** to close the Slide Transition dialog box.
5. Play the slide show to view your visual effects. Remember to click the mouse button to move to the next slide. You must also click the mouse button to view each cascading bullet.
6. Save the slide show as **SHURTRAN** and leave it on the screen for the next exercise.

Controlling Slide Advance

The Slide Transition dialog box also lets you control how the slide show plays. The option buttons in the Advance area of the dialog box let you choose Manual or Timed advance. Manual advance is the method you have used so far—you must manually advance each slide by clicking the mouse button. The Timed option advances each slide according to a time delay that you set in the Seconds to Delay box. When you select Timed and a delay time, Presentations plays your slide show for you, including cascading the bullets.

EXERCISE 10-2

Add Timed advances to your slide show.

1. Choose **Transition** from the **Slide** menu to open the Slide Transition dialog box again.
2. Begin with Slide 1 and click the **Timed** option button. Set a delay of 3 seconds by clicking the up arrow next to the Seconds to Delay box.
3. Set timed delays for the other slides and click **OK.**
4. Play the slide show again and observe how Presentations advances the slides and cascades the bullets for you automatically.
5. Save the slide show and leave it on the screen for the next exercise.

The Slide List View

You will find the Slide List view especially helpful at this stage of preparing your slide show. The Slide List view shows you all the slides in your presentation by title along with the type of transition (if any) and how you propose to advance through your slides (Figure 10–2). Any changes you make in your slides are reflected in this list.

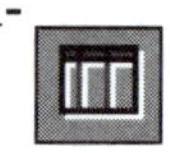
Slide List View

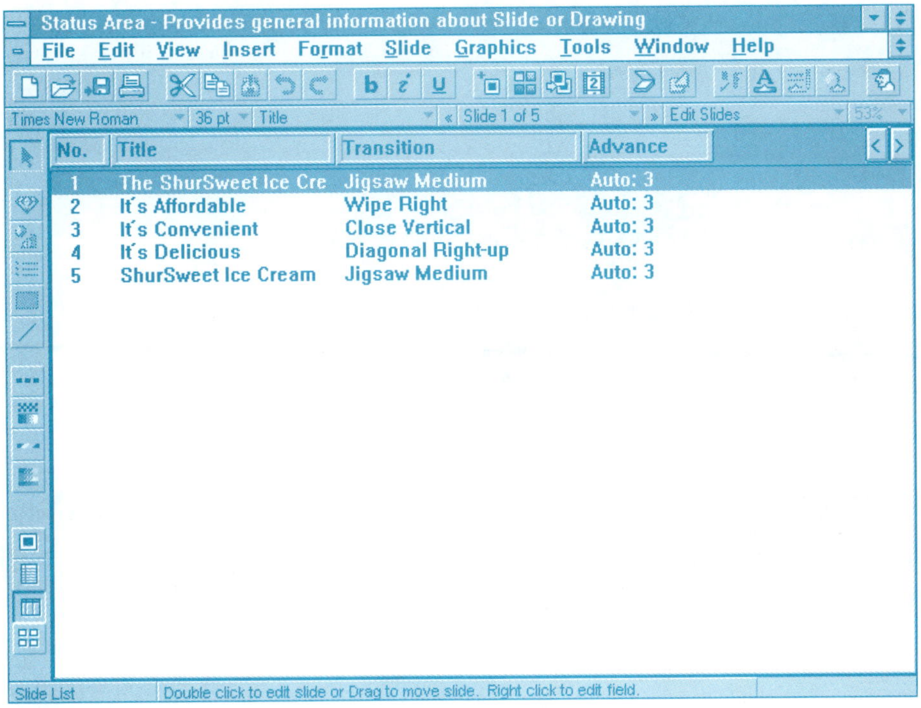

Figure 10–2
Slide List view screen

ADDING SOUND TO YOUR SLIDE SHOW

The Slide Transition dialog box also contains a Sound button you can use to add sound effects to your slide show, if your system is set up for sound. Presentations provides three **.WAV** sound files and 93 MIDI sound files you can use as desired. You can add a different sound effect to each slide.

To add sound effects to your slides:

- Choose **Transition** from the **Slide** menu.
- Use the arrow buttons to choose the slide to which you want to add sound.
- Click the **Sound** button to open the Sound dialog box shown in Figure 10–3 (on p. 138).

The Standard Sound Files area contains two text fields, one for selecting Digital (**.WAV**) files and one for selecting MIDI files (if you have a multimedia system that can play MIDI files).

To select the sound file you want to use:

- Click the file button at the end of either the Digital text box or the MIDI text box. The Select File dialog box appears with a list of available files, as shown in Figure 10–4 (on p. 138).
- Click a file in the list to choose it, then click **OK.**

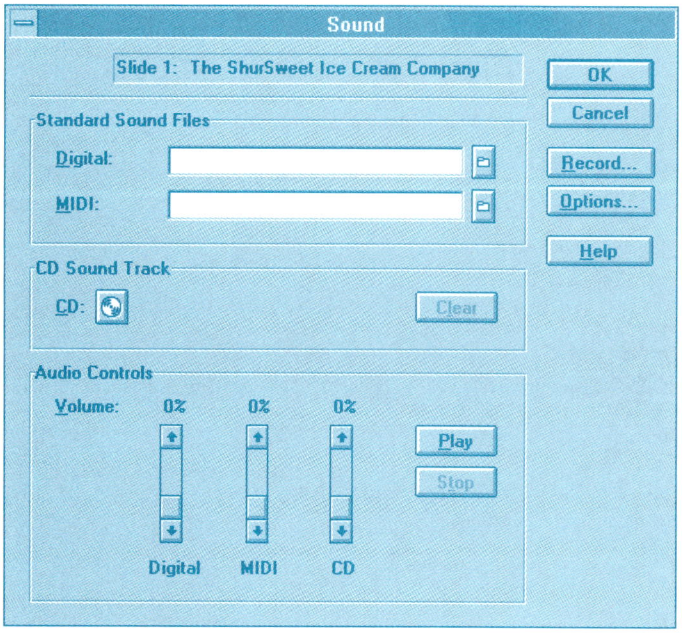

Figure 10-3
The Sound dialog box

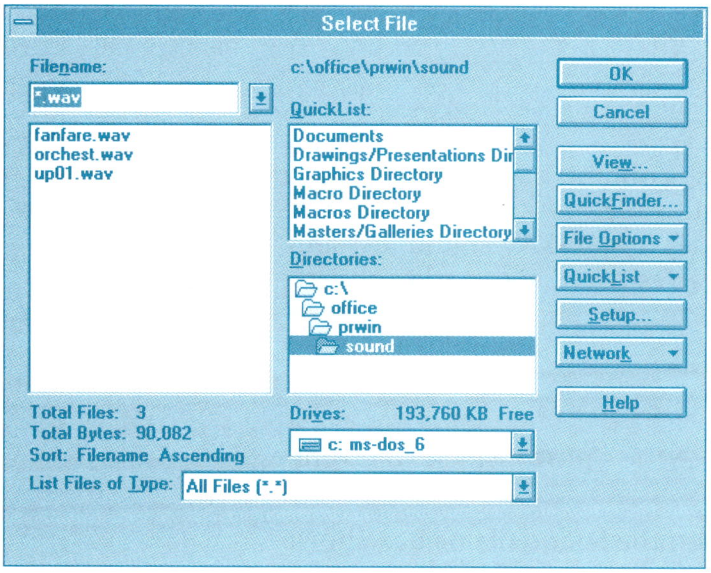

Figure 10-4
The Select File dialog box

When either the Digital or MIDI text field contains a file name, you can click the Play button to listen to the sound file and make sure it is appropriate. You can select and play sound files until you find exactly the right file to get your message across. When you have found the right sound effect, click the OK buttons in the Sound and Slide Transition dialog boxes. The sound effect will play as the slide is displayed. Some sound effects are very long and will play until the slide is removed from the screen.

EXERCISE 10-3

Optional Exercise: If your system is configured to play sounds, add sounds to your slide show.

1. Choose **Transition** from the **Slide** menu.
2. Use the arrow buttons to select Slide 1.
3. Click the **Sound** button. The Sound dialog box appears.
4. Click the file button at the end of the Digital text field. The Select File dialog box appears.
5. Select **FANFARE.WAV** from the Filename list box and click **OK.**
6. Click the **Play** button and listen to the fanfare.
7. Click **OK** *twice* to return to the Slide Editor view.
8. Play the slide show. When the first slide displays, you should hear the fanfare.
9. Save the slide show and close the file.
10. Exit Presentations.

MAKING THE PRESENTATION

After you have created your basic slide show, you can begin making final preparations for your presentation. The way you present yourself and your information will determine how successful your overall presentation will be.

Being well-prepared is your best chance for success. There is no substitute for advance planning and preparation. Follow the guidelines below to make sure you are ready for your presentation.

1. *Know your material.* Make sure you are completely familiar with everything you are about to say.
2. *Conduct trial runs without an audience.* Become familiar with the room you will be presenting in. Be aware of any obstacles, such as pillars in the room, that might interfere with the audience's view of your slide show. Make sure you can read the text and distinguish the art in your presentation from any spot in the room. Be sure that your equipment is working properly and that you know how to fix any problems that might arise.
3. *Conduct trial runs with an audience.* Make sure you can be heard anywhere in the room. Make sure your test audience can read and understand your slides and any charts and graphics you have included.

As you rehearse, reexamine your charts to make sure they fulfill your purpose. Make sure the color combinations on the charts emphasize the proper feature so your audience will get the message you want to send. Make sure your presentation is understandable and accurate.

Try not to use any "crutches" to help you make your presentation. Try to establish rapport with your audience so they will be on your side. *Occasionally* injecting a bit of humor can help your audience identify with you.

You should be familiar enough with your presentation that you can give the presentation without written notes. Maintain eye contact with your audience throughout the entire presentation. Enunciate clearly, speak slowly, and speak loudly enough that people at the back of the room can hear you.

Remember, what you have to say is important, so don't rush through your presentation. Take your time. Emphasize and restate important aspects of your presentation. Give your audience time to interpret your slides and digest what you say. A good rule to follow is that a slide should be projected on the screen for at least 10 seconds.

Speakers who use notes or written materials are often not as effective as those speakers who speak "off the cuff." If you have rehearsed your material sufficiently, you should always know what comes next. If your presentation has been well-planned, your slides will emphasize the important aspects of your speech and will help you remember the key points of your presentation.

If you appear bored and dull, your audience will be bored and dull. Enthusiasm breeds enthusiasm. If *you* are enthusiastic about your material, your audience will be, too. Good presenters believe in themselves and their presentations. Their confidence shines through!

ACTIVITIES

TRUE/FALSE

In the blank space before each sentence, place a **T** if the statement is true and an **F** if it is false.

______ 1. You can add both visual and sound effects to your slides.

______ 2. Visual effects can help keep your audience focused on your message.

______ 3. With the *Box* transition, the screen breaks up into small blocks as it is removed from or added to the screen.

______ 4. With the *Spots* transition, the screen breaks up into spots as it is removed from or added to the screen.

______ 5. After you have finished creating the slides, you probably need no further preparation before giving your presentation.

COMPLETION

Fill in the blank.

1. You use the ________________ dialog box to add visual effects to your slides.
2. The ________________ option displays bullets one at a time.
3. ________________ advance lets you control the slide show with the mouse.
4. You use the ________________ view to display a list of the slides in your presentation and the type of transition you have specified for each.
5. You use the ________________ dialog box to add sound effects to your slide show.

R E V I E W

REVIEW EXERCISE 10-1

The ShurSweet annual report presentation is nearly complete. Add the final touches in this exercise.

1. Start Presentations and retrieve **ANNREPT4.SHW** from your data disk.
2. Add appropriate transitions to the slides. Remember not to use too many different kinds. Add Timed advance to the slide show so it will play automatically.
3. If your system is able to play sounds, add appropriate sound effects to the slides.
4. Review the entire slide show and check that the slides you have created are consistent with one another and present a uniform "look." Modify the slides as necessary.
5. Check the slides in the Slide Sorter view to make sure they are in the correct order. Note that some of the slides do not have titles. These are the Background slides you added to prepare charts on.
6. Switch to Outliner view and add appropriate titles for the untitled slides.
7. Change to the Slide List view to make sure you have transitions and advance options for each slide.
8. Play the slide show.
9. Save the slide show as **FINALRPT.** Print the slide show as a handout with six slides per page and no background.
10. Close the file and exit Presentations.

Glossary

Appearance Character enhancements similar to font styles, such as regular, bold, italic, and bold italic.
Ascending order A method of arranging data in order from lowest value to highest value. Use this order if you want to stress the lowest values.
Axis title A label that provides descriptive information about the type of data plotted on an axis.

Background A predesigned graphic for a master set that provides a uniform look for all the slides in a slide show.
Bar chart A chart that represents sets of data as bars on X- and Y-axes. A bar chart is particularly good for comparing quantities.
Bullets Small symbols (•, ◆, ➢, etc.) that mark the beginning of a line of text in a bullet chart. Bullet charts clearly mark each point in a list of entries.

Cascade bullets A transition effect that allows you to display bullet lists one bullet at a time.
Check box A small box you click within a dialog box to select an option. You can select multiple check boxes at one time.
Clicking Pressing and releasing the left mouse button.
Clip art Predesigned graphic images you can insert into your slides. Presentations refers to clip art as "QuickArt."
Clipboard A storage area in memory common to all Windows applications. You use the clipboard to move or copy data from one place or document to another.
Closing a file Removing the active file from the screen.
Command button Small, rectangular boxes with labels such as OK, Cancel, and Help that you click within a dialog box to access a command.
Connectors The lines that connect the boxes in an organization chart.
Constraining A feature that lets you control aspects of each object type as you draw. To constrain an object while you draw it, hold down the **Shift** key. For example, pressing **Shift** while you drag an ellipse results in a perfect circle. Pressing **Shift** while using the Line tool lets you draw exactly horizontal, vertical, or 45° angle lines.
Copying Placing a duplicate of selected data in another location, leaving the original data intact.
Cursor A blinking vertical line in a text box that indicates the position where text will be deleted or inserted.

Datasheet A spreadsheet-like guide you use to enter text and numerical data for charts.
Dependent variable A quantity that can change based on another value. The dependent variable is plotted on the X-axis.
Descending order A method of arranging data in order from highest value to lowest value. Use this order if you want to stress the highest values.
Deselect To turn off selection.
Dialog box A small window you use to give Presentations specific instructions about how to operate. Dialog boxes appear when Presentations needs you to enter more information before it can complete an action. Dialog boxes can contain command buttons, option buttons, check boxes, text boxes, and list boxes.
Double-clicking Pressing the left mouse button twice in rapid succession.

Exploding Separating a pie slice from the whole pie to emphasize it.

Figure editor A feature you use to make changes to graphic objects on your slides. You can change or even delete parts of a figure while leaving other parts intact.
Fill The pattern or color within a closed figure such as a rectangle or closed curve.
Font A set of characters and numbers in one particular size and design. Each font has a name, such as Times New Roman or Arial.
Frame The Y-axis line, the X-axis line, the top line, and the right line (if the chart type has a right line) that enclose a chart.

Grid The series of horizontal and vertical lines that mark increments on the X- and Y-axes.

Handles Small boxes at the corners and edges of selected objects you use to size, rotate, or skew the objects.

Icon A small picture that represents a command. You can click an icon to execute a command without accessing menus.

Independent variable Data whose value does not depend on another variable. The independent variable is plotted on the Y-axis.

Justification The way text lines up relative to the edge of the text box. Left-justified text aligns at the left edge of the text box. Center-justified text is aligned at the center of the text box, with equal space to the left and right edge. Right-justified text aligns at the right edge of the text box.

Legend The "key" to reading a chart. The legend tells you what the colors of the bars or pie slices, or the styles and/or colors of the lines, represent.
Line Outlines of closed objects or lines drawn with the Line tool.
Line chart A data chart that represents data values as points on a line plotted on X- and Y-axes.
Linked pie A pie chart with a slice linked to another pie representating a breakdown of the contents of the slice.
List box A dialog box field that contains several predetermined options from which you can choose.

Master set A set of predesigned backgrounds and templates you can use to give your slides a uniform look.
Menu A list of commands you can choose from. You access menus through the menu bar near the top of the Presentations window.
Menu bar A line near the top of the Presentations working screen that contains the names of several lists of commands. You click on the name of a menu to open its list of commands.
Moving Removing data from one location and placing it in another location.

Opening a file Retrieving a file from the disk where it is stored.
Option button A small, round button you click to select options in a dialog box. You can select only one option button at a time. Option buttons are sometimes called "radio buttons."
Organization chart A chart that indicates the relationship of individuals in an organization.
Outliner A view in Presentations you use to create outlines.
Overlay A transition effect that lets you display one slide on top of another.

Pie chart A data chart that represents an entire group of data as a circle divided into proportional sections based on some type of distinguishing characteristic.
Power Bar A line of buttons near the top of the Presentations working screen you use to access commonly used functions without accessing menus.

Presentation graphics Software programs designed to help you create effective visual presentations, create slide presentations, overhead transparencies, printed handouts, and screen shows on the computer screen.
Presentations A Novell software package designed to help you create presentation graphics.
Proportional pies Pie charts sized according to the numbers entered in the datasheet. The chart whose data values total the most is drawn the largest. The chart whose data values total the least is drawn the smallest, and so on.

QuickArt Presentations' name for predesigned graphic images you can insert into your slides. QuickArt is sometimes called "clip art."

Radio button A small, round button you click to select options in a dialog box. You can select only one radio button at a time. Radio button is another name for an option button.
Rotating Turning an object from its original position around an invisible axis in the center of the object.

Select To highlight text or an object that you wish to edit.
Size The size of the characters in points. There are 72 points to 1 inch, so 12-point type is one-sixth of an inch high.
Skewing Distorting a graphic so it appears slanted.
Slide Editor view A Presentations screen you use to enter/edit the data on your slides.
Slide List view A Presentations screen you use to display thumbnails of your slides and the transition effects assigned to each.
Slide show A set of presentation graphics designed for displaying to an audience.
Slide Sorter view A Presentations screen you use to view/rearrange the order of your slides.
Staff position On an organization chart, a support person for another position in the organization chart. Staff persons include assistants and secretaries.
Style Character enhancements such as regular, bold, italic, and bold italic. A particular font might not have all these styles available. You can use only one style at a time.
Subordinate position On an organization chart, a position that reports to a higher position.
Superior position On an organization chart, a position that has other positions reporting to it.

Tables Sets of data entries arranged in rows and columns.
Template A predesigned layout for each slide type in a master set.

Text box A dialog box field that requires you to type information. This is often the only way to enter some kinds of information.
Text charts Charts that convey textual information instead of statistical information. Presentations provides two types of text charts: bullet charts and data charts.
Text editor A white box with a heavy blue border you use to edit text on your slides. It contains a cursor (the blinking vertical line) that indicates where your text will be inserted or deleted.
Text slides Slides that contain text, including title slides, bullet chart slides, data chart slides, and combinations of these types. The text for text slides is entered into text blocks that appear on the working screen. These text blocks can be supplied in predetermined positions by a template, or you can create and position your own text blocks.
Thumbnails Reduced-size versions of slides used to display several slides on a screen or to print several slides on a page.
Tick marks The small lines that extend from the axis labels to the axes themselves.
Title slides Slides you use to present your titles and subtitles.
Toolbar A set of icons near the top of the Presentations working screen. You use these icons to access frequently used commands without using menus.
Tool palette A set of icons in the left margin of the Presentations working screen. You use these icons to access certain drawing commands without using menus.
Transition The way a slide show changes from one slide to another.
Trend The way a value changes over time.

Views Screens in Presentations that allow you to look at your slide show in different ways.

X-axis A horizontal line divided into segments on which data is plotted.
XY chart A chart that uses a grid with horizontal (X) and vertical (Y) axes to determine placement of the data points. XY charts include bar charts, line charts, scatter charts, area charts, etc. While the appearance of each of these types of charts is different, they all use the X- and Y-axes to determine the placement of their data points.

Y-axis A vertical line divided into segments based on the variable to be plotted on it.

Index

D

E

F

P

Q

R

S

T

U

V

W

X

Y